Getting More From
Math
Manipulatives

Getting More From
Math
Manipulatives

Strategies, Lessons, Activities, and Assessment

By Birgitta Corneille

SCHOLASTIC
PROFESSIONAL BOOKS

New York • Toronto • London • Auckland • Sydney

To Liisa, Edward, Marc and Erik

Cover design by Vincent Ceci and Jaime Lucero
Cover photograph by Donnelly Marks
Interior design by Vincent Ceci and Drew Hires
Interior illustrations by James Graham Hale

ISBN # 0-590-27050-8
Copyright © 1995 by Birgitta Corneille
All rights reserved.
Printed in the U.S.A.

12 11 10 9 8 7 6 5 4 3 2 1   1 2 3 4 5 6 / 9

Contents

Preface

When I began teaching mathematics to elementary school children, I often browsed through the textbooks and workbooks that teachers were asked to use with their students. I was disappointed to see how little attention was devoted in those mathematics books to manipulatives as tools for learning.

Over the years, I had grown aware of the power of manipulatives to convey math concepts to young children. I felt that children's experimentations with manipulatives—from two-sided counters to geoblocks—would create in youngsters a sound understanding of the number system and show the connection between concrete materials and algorithms. As a result, I began creating my own manipulatives for use in the classrooms. It was a learning process for me as well as for my students.

At first, the main manipulatives I used were the base-10 blocks. It did not take me long to realize, though, that the blocks alone did not "teach" the children place value and regrouping the way I had hoped. I found that I needed to review or reteach these concepts every year.

After experimenting with a variety of homemade materials and their corresponding activities, I began to understand that children needed lots of classroom instruction to construct their knowledge of place value. Before long, I replaced the base-10 blocks with snap cubes or interlocking cubes. I found that the latter materials encouraged children to form groupings with which they felt more comfortable. (Initially, children grouped by 2, then by 5. Once the quantities I presented became larger, children grouped by 10, and later by 10 and by 100.)

Although I used a basal textbook as part of my mathematics program, I found that children's conceptual understanding came from their explorations with manipulatives and from the decisions they made as they solved problems with those tools. In those early years of teaching, I learned the importance of allowing children ample time to make connections between their explorations with manipulatives and symbolic notation. If the connections were not made, I realized, the experiences the children acquired in class and the examples on the pages of the textbook ran on parallel tracks. The children would not see how the two were related.

I encouraged the children to use the basal textbook as a resource and a reinforcement for skills. Once the children understood and became comfortable with symbolic notation, they delighted in showing their knowledge of mathematics by completing certain workbook exercises. Throughout the day, children also took pleasure from other activities that displayed their growing skills, from estimating to doing mental math.

It is my hope that the activities in this book will inspire you to use manipulatives to a greater extent and will help you to create a sound, mathematically rewarding classroom for your young learners.

Introduction

Manipulatives Began in Ancient Times

Concrete materials have been used since ancient times. Primitive humans used sticks and pebbles to show quantity. In those days, numerical symbols did not yet exist. Traders used concrete objects to keep track of items being traded or to communicate the price of items being sold. They kept a record of the transactions by using a one-to-one correspondence ("One pebble stands for one apple"), then combining the sticks and pebbles to get the total. Interestingly enough, young children use the same method today!

In earlier eras, paper was nonexistent, rare, or unavailable to the masses. One way that records were kept, was by making scratches or notches in wood, dirt, or bone, or by tying knots in strings. These different records can be observed in the wood blocks of the British, the clay tablets of the Babylonians, and the quipus of the Peruvian Indians.

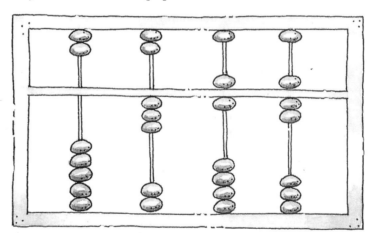

One of the most sophisticated uses of concrete materials was the Chinese use of an abacus. An abacus shows place value as well as grouping by 1s and 5s within each place. This tool was so efficient that many consider it the first calculator.

As years went on, concrete materials were followed by the use of finger numbers (for example, 2 fingers show the price or quantity of 2). Since 10 is the largest quantity that can be shown without any difficulty, different cultures invented various combinations to show larger numbers. In fact, finger numbers are still used today by traders on the floor of many stock markets.

In the past, pictures were also employed to show quantity, such as in the Egyptian numeration system. In that system

 stands for one, for 10, and 🌀 for 100.

Egyptians grouped their pictorial representations by 10, but their system did not have a place value component. (The pictorial representations do not have value depending on their placements. The 1s can come before or after the 10s or 100s.)

It was not until the discovery and use of zero by the Hindus and Arabs that the placement of the symbol or digits received value. Egyptian and Roman numeral systems do not require a symbol for zero, since you total the the symbols. For instance, Roman numerals MXXX show 1000 + 10 + 10 + 10 = 1030. Egyptian numerals show 100 + 100 + 1 + 1, or 202. The introduction of zero into our numeral system indicates a missing power of ten and the placement of the digits gives the digits their value. For instance, in 305 the zero shows that there no tens while the 3 shows that there are 3 hundreds and the 5 shows that there are 5 ones. If we do not have a zero, the number shows 3 tens and 5 ones, or 35. As the Hindu-Arabic numeration system gained popularity, place value became important. This occurred in India some time before A.D. 800 and in Europe during the 15th century.

As children explore mathematical concepts today, they follow much the same progression as in the evolution of the development of numbers.

Using Manipulatives with Children

Children come to kindergarten or first grade with a great deal of number knowledge. They use their everyday experiences to construct sophisticated math. For instance, children count up from 1 and frequently count back from 10 without much difficulty. (In this case, they might mimic behavior they have observed as they watched spacecraft take off on television. And, with the current popularity of microwave ovens, many children can also count back from 59. Some children will note that the timer first shows 1:00, then 59.)

Children can also tell the difference between numbers showing a quantity, such as 5 apples, and numbers representing an idea, such as 5 for a bus route. They also realize that the 5 in "5 years old" does not mean the same as the quantity expressed in "5 apples."

This knowledge has developed over time. Children have made the connection between their concrete experiences and their conceptual understanding. Working with manipulatives helps children move from the concrete to the pictorial to the abstract, or symbolic.

Helping Children Explore Mathematics with Manipulatives

Within the last century, educators such as Maria Montessori and Zoltan Dienes observed children as they learned and played. Montessori and Dienes began to realize how important it was for children to go through stages of concrete experiences. The stages helped children better understand the relationships between their actions, concrete manipulations, and symbolic notations. These educators developed a variety of manipulatives that help children relate their concrete experiences to mathematics.

As a result of their research, Montessori and Dienes developed materials to enhance student learning. In the early 1900s, Maria Montessori created a variety of self-paced learning materials. Her method and materials have influenced early childhood education today.

In the mid-20th century, Zoltan Dienes developed base-10 blocks. He saw the difficulties children had with understanding quantity and relating quantity to standard algorithms and regrouping (that is, borrowing in subtraction and carrying in addition). The blocks helped in that area.

We, as teachers, owe a great deal to the early work of these educators.

Connecting Experiences with Manipulatives to Symbolic Notation

Children need many opportunities to share information with each other and to express their attempts at solving problems. ("I checked off each shape after I traced it. Then I knew I had traced all the faces.")

They also need to be introduced to symbolism. Children must learn the meaning of symbols and understand how the symbols relate to their adventures with concrete materials. The ideas in this book will give you some suggestions for conveying these concepts.

Children Working Together

When children in primary grades use manipulatives, they should work in pairs. Later, as they become accustomed to working together, children can work in larger groups. For example, groups of 4 are acceptable toward the end of second grade or in third grade. Groups of 3 might sometimes become problematic, depending on children's personalities.

Grouping children in pairs or small groups encourages children to talk about what they are doing. Sharing knowledge with a partner is less overwhelming than sharing information with the whole class or a larger group. In addition, when children work with a partner, they are more likely to persist with the activity.

Math Journals

A mathematics journal serves much the same purpose as a reading response journal. Even when children are too young to write conventional letters and numbers, they should be encouraged to keep journals in math.

About what should they write? During lessons at the beginning of the year, ask children to show, through drawing, their favorite math activity for the day or for the week. If time permits, children can explain what the activity was and why they liked it. The names of the activities can be written underneath the picture by you or another adult. The frequency with which children write in their math journals depends on the time available.

As children learn to write, they can write about a variety of topics, such as the following:
• what they learned about a specific concept
• what they really like about a concept
• an area with which they might have difficulties
• generalizations they have about different concepts.
Drawings and illustrations of the manipulatives should be included.

MANAGEMENT TIP
Show children how to make their math journals by folding several pieces of paper in half. Then make a cover from a piece of colorful construction paper. Staple the booklet on one side.

Children can write their names on the cover and illustrate their work inside.

In primary grades, children should be encouraged to use inventive spelling, that is, use their knowledge of phonics to sound out and write the words. Children might then read their journal entry to each other or to an adult. If children want the correct spelling, a spelling list can be created on the chalkboard and added to as time permits. Spelling should not, however, be overemphasized.

A math journal can be created for each concept the children cover in math (addition or geometry, for example) or for the entire year ("My First Grade Journal"). At the end of the year the math journals will show the children what they learned in mathematics that year. It truly will be their math book. Journals can also be sent home periodically to be shared with family members.

Moving On

It is important that children have ample opportunity to become familiar with the various concrete manipulatives. This involves a great deal of playing with, sorting, and comparing of tools. Before children can use the manipulatives in mathematics, they need to find out how the items "work," how they can be used for building, how they can be used to make designs, and how they can be used to make informal patterns.

Let's begin with snap cubes.

MANAGEMENT TIP

To introduce the idea of writing in mathematics, begin slowly. Whenever the children have done something noteworthy, encourage them to draw a picture of what they have learned. Then have them write a few words about the concepts or ideas. One or two lines are sufficient. Encourage children to write a little more each time.

Chapter 1

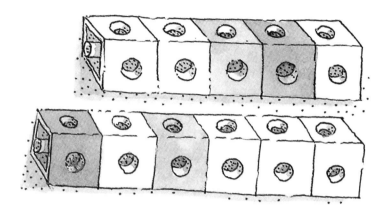

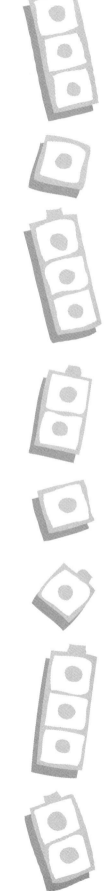

Snap Cubes or Interlocking Cubes

Children like to work with snap cubes. In elementary school mathematics, snap cubes are conducive to sorting, especially by color. As time goes on, the cubes can also become representational. That is, they can be used to represent an idea (such as the number of children who like that color), an object (an apple), or a place (the block corner of the classroom).

This type of representation can be illustrated by displaying information in a physical bar graph, using snap cubes as the bars. In this case, the snap cubes can give two sets of information. The colors of the snap cube can represent different classroom centers, while each snap cube represents a child. Every time the children visit a classroom center, they add a snap cube to the other snap cubes there or begin a new bar, showing that they visited the center.

During sharing time the children bring the different snap cube rods with them. Youngsters can compare the different snap cube bars, analyzing the information each conveys. For instance, if the bar representing the block corner is longer than the bars from the other centers, children will see that more students visited the block corner than the other centers.

Counting

Children can also use snap cubes for comparing, counting, or partitioning quantities. Since snap cubes are easily attached to each other, children can line up rods of cubes and compare them, noting, for example, which have at least 5 cubes and which rod is longest.

By snapping the cubes together, youngsters can make groups, such as groups of 2s or 5s. Since the cubes have been snapped together, the whole set moves as a unit. (This is not the case with some other concrete materials, such as beads or coins.) As children count the groups, they can organize the information more easily ("5, 10, 15, 20").

Skip Counting

Cubes snapped together encourage skip counting. When skip counting by 2s, the children skip one number when rote counting. For instance, with 2, 4, 6, 8, the odd numbers are skipped. (Sometimes the terminology "skip counting by 2," confuses children, since they associate the term to mean "skipping 2 numbers.") Using the cubes alleviates confusion because the children can place the cubes in groups of 2 and see that they are counting 2 cubes at a time.

As the numbers get larger, it is important that children use some kind of skip counting because counting by 1s is exhausting. When counting by 1s, young children sometimes lose count if they are interrupted. If, however, the cubes are grouped into 5s or 10s, children only need to count the small groups of 5 and 10, rather than the whole group of objects. They can then count the total by skip counting by 5 or 10.

When grouping and counting by 10, children begin to understand our base-10 numeration system and internalize the place value concept through their recordings.

Writing and Sharing Mathematics

After much counting has been done, the connections between children's pictorial representations of their work and symbolic notation needs to be introduced. For instance, if children have counted a quantity such as 37 using groupings by 5 and skip counting the total, the following connections can be shown to them:

| 5 | 10 | 15 | 20 | 25 | 30 | 35 | 36 | 37 |

Another way to show the same total is to group the 5s to form 10s:

| 10 | 20 | 30 | 35 | 36 | 37 |

As the children become more familiar with grouping and combining, the next step would be to show the following:

$$10 + 10 + 10 + 5 + 2 = 37$$

The important part is to connect the skip counting process to what happens symbolically. This is best shown through repeated addition such as the one shown above. The number sentence needs to be broken down into steps, such as $10 + 10 = 20$, and then $20 + 10 = 30$. As the children become accustomed to the symbolic notation, they break down a process into parts on their own.

Throughout their explorations, children need to record their work as well as verbally explain the concepts. Encouraging children to record their explorations and discoveries helps them move through a process of connecting their concrete explorations to symbolic expressions. Children reach the stage of symbolic expression at different times. Listening to classmates explain the mathematical connections and processes they discovered will help everyone's mathematical growth.

Partitioning and Combining

After children have had many opportunities to count different quantities using snap cubes, they also need to experience the different ways numbers can be shown. For instance, they might have counted the quantity of 16 by 1s, by 2s and even by 5s. They now need to concentrate on other ways 16 can be shown. They might snap the 16 cubes together and then randomly break the rod into 2. Here again the important part is to encourage the children to record the different combinations and follow up with questions about whether or not they have all the different combinations. When children break rods apart, the combinations they get might, at times, be the same. This is also important for them to talk about.

Another way children approach partitioning is by using 2 different colors of snap cubes. Each color shows an addend. Here, for example, are just a few combinations children might construct with 16 snap cubes.

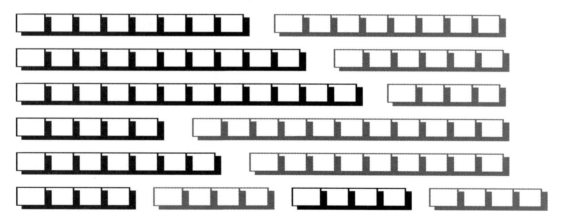

Children usually combine the 2 colors without any apparent organization or understanding that there is a finite number of possible combinations.

Organized Lists

During early lessons, the lists children create are not necessarily organized. You, as teacher, can help in this area by asking questions such as, "Can you tell if there are any other combinations you can make?" and then, "How did you know that one was missing?" Children begin to create patterns of existing combinations and missing ones until they see the organization emerging. Their lists might look something like this:

0 + 16, 1 + 15, 2 + 14, 3 + 13 4 + 12, 5 + 11, 6 + 10, 7 + 9, 8 + 8, 9 + 7, 10

+ 6, 11 + 5, 12 + 4, 13 + 3, 14 + 2, 15 + 1, 16 + 0

Storing the Manipulatives

Since snap cubes are used for sorting and counting, they need to be stored in a large container. A large container such as a shoe box works best. Be sure to label the storage container. Children can refer to the label when writing about their explorations.

A large, open container allows children to return their snap cubes without taking time to separate the snap cubes into single cubes. At the beginning of lessons, children can also carry the groups of snap cubes to their desks with little difficulty. Few single cubes will fall to the floor.

When the snap cubes are all kept together, the sorting activities suggest themselves. In the beginning it might be by color but after the children have had opportunities to play and work with them, the sorting activity might be by 1s, 2s, 5s, and 10s. This simply means that children have a tendency to sort by the most obvious attribute, in this case, color. As they continue to play with the snap cubes, many of the cubes will remain snapped together. When children then sort, they might sort the snap cubes according to quantity in the rods. For instance, all the rods showing less than 10 and all rods showing more than 10.

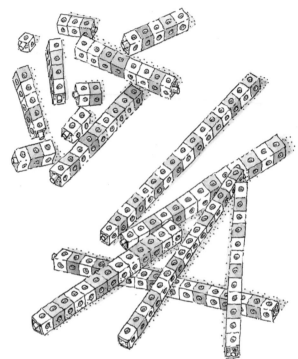

Activities with Snap Cubes or Interlocking Cubes

Counting
Purpose: Counting and grouping
Grouping of Students: Individual or pairs
Materials: 20-50 snap cubes per individual or pair, paper for recording
NCTM Standards: Mathematics as Communication, Number Sense, and Numeration
Directions:
1. Invite children to take a variety of snap cubes. Ask youngsters to estimate how many they have.
2. Have children count their cubes and record how they counted and the quantity. Ask them to compare their estimates with the actual number.
3. Ask the children to switch cubes with another pair or individual.
4. Have the children estimate their new quantities and write them down. Ask children to count the cubes, suggesting that this time they count them in a new way.

5. Now have youngsters compare their answers with those of the individual or pair that had the cubes first.

6. Encourage the children to draw or write how they counted. Then have them generalize what the difference was between their first counting and the second. Which way was easier? Faster? More accurate?

Assessment

Observe as children estimate the number of cubes. Some youngsters will see that there are a lot of cubes and give a number that they consider large, such as 100. Others will estimate the number of cubes being more or less than a certain number, such as more or less than 10 cubes. Still others will look at the cubes and count out 5 cubes and visually skip count the total by approximately 5 cubes at a time.

As children count the cubes, notice that some children will feel comfortable counting by 1s. When they are asked to count another way, they might group the cubes, but not in equal groups. They will continue counting the cubes by 1s.

In the first activity, some students will count by 1s. In the following activity, they will group the cubes into equal groups, but still count the cubes by 1s. During the first activity, some children will count the cubes by 2s and skip count by 2s. In the second activity, they will group the cubes in larger groups, and again, skip count by that number.

As often as possible, ask the children to tell you how they counted and the difference between the ways.

Grouping; Adding One Or Subtracting One

Purpose: Counting, odd/even patterns, adding and subtracting 1
Grouping of Students: Pairs
Materials: About 20 snap cubes per pair, paper for record recording
NCTM Standards: Mathematics as Communication, Mathematics as Problem Solving, Whole Number Computation
Directions:

1. Ask pairs of children to take about 20 snap cubes. Have them guess if they have an odd or an even number.

2. Invite children to group the snap cubes by 2s to see if the number is odd or even and to count the cubes. How many do they have? Do all of the snap cubes form pairs? Ask children to record their answers.

3. What will happen if they add one more snap cube? Is the number odd or even? How many do they have now? How did they get the answer? Did they count or add? Have the children record their answers.

4. Suggest that children remove one cube from the original set. Is the number odd or even? How many do they have now? How did they get the answer? Did they count or subtract? Have the children record the answers.

5. This activity can also be done grouping the snap cubes in groups of 3s, 4s, and 5s when children are comfortable with larger numbers and with skip counting. Have them deal with the whole groups. How many groups do they have? Do they have an odd or even number of groups?

Assessment

As you observe how children determine odd or even, you will probably notice that some children guess the answers without knowing what either word means.

Some children will snap the cubes into pairs of 2s to determine odd or even. Some will count the cubes and determine odd or even from the answer. Have children share their methods with each other.

As children add or remove one cube from their original number, observe how they determine odd/even patterns. Some youngsters will regroup the total by 2s and look at whether or not the cubes form pairs. Some children will visually add the cube or remove the cube from the previous total and decide whether or not the new cube or removal of a cube would make even pairs. Some will use their knowledge of numbers and the pattern of our number system and determine whether or not they have an even/odd total.

Also observe how children determine the total number of cubes. Some will recount the cubes starting with one. Others will group the cubes by 2s and skip count the total. Still others will consider the previous total and add one or subtract one.

Staircase Patterns for Addition and Subtraction

Purpose: Adding and subtracting facts to 10
Grouping of Students: Pairs
Materials: Prepared sets of 10 red snap cubes and 10 blue snap cubes per pair, paper for recording
NCTM Standards: Mathematical Connections, Mathematics as Communication, Mathematics as Problem Solving, Concepts of Whole Number Computation
Directions

1. Ask children to collect their sets of snap cubes. Ask them to choose 1 color and snap the cubes together. How many cubes do they have? Have them draw a picture of their snap cube rod. Invite them to write down on the side of their paper the number of snap cubes.

2. Tell the children that they need to have 10 cubes at all times in their rod, but the cubes need not be the same color. Model for children. Show a rod with 1 blue snap cube and 9 red snap cubes. Ask children to record the numbers of their rods.

3. Ask the children to continue showing and recording the different ways to have a rod of 10 snap cubes, using 1 or 2 colors.

4. Ask the children if they have all representations of 10 or if there are some representations missing. Suggest that they create an organized list to see if all representations have been recorded.

5. Can youngsters suggest how to show these rods using a subtraction sentence? Hold up 8 red cubes. Ask how many blue cubes they would need to make a 10-cube rod. Model the children's responses using a number sentence: 10 - 8 = 2. Have the children return to their records and write subtraction sentences for their different addition sentences.

6. At the end of the activity, give the children an opportunity to share their findings.

7. In most cases, children will find it difficult to write addition or subtraction sentences for rods with one color. For instance, 10 red cubes can be written 10 = 10 + 0 or 10 = 10 - 0. If you like, you might want to model these sentences for the children or wait until someone in the class suggests it.

Assessment

As children record their investigations with the 10s rods using two colors, some will record their findings pictorially.

Others will use a combination of pictures and numbers. Still other boys and girls will use pictures but will also include number sentences.

Observe how youngsters organize the information. Some children will combine the cubes without any organization. Some children will start out without organizing their methods. They will begin to organize the representations as they try to determine if they have all of the possible combinations. Some children will approach the activity methodically by exchanging the color of 1 cube for the other color.

Two-Colored Counters

At first, counters are used for—counting. Children use them in much the same way as snap cubes, that is, for one-to-one correspondence. ("This chip stands for one, that chip stands for two.") "One-to-one correspondence" means that children assign one number to each individual counter they count. They touch or move the counter to the side in order not to recount any of the previously counted objects.

Children like to use counters. Because of their size and shape, children can grab quite a few in a handful.

Counters can be used in addition and subtraction as well as in counting. When working in pairs or groups, boys and girls can separate their pile of counters into 2 or more groups, estimating the size of each. This encourages approximation and checking estimates. After the counters have been grouped, counting the groups will be an important activity. No youngster wants to have less than the others.

Adding and Subtracting

When children use counters to model addition activities, the color of the counters makes no difference. The children essentially model the 2 or more parts the activity calls for and then combine the groups into a total. The same is true for subtraction activities. Youngsters start with the total and separate it into parts. One part is disposed of while the other becomes the answer to the problem.

After children have done combining and partitioning activities, they should record them. These activities need to follow the same progression as with snap cubes. That is, children need to make connections between what they are doing and what they show symbolically. Initially, the activity should take children through three stages: concrete, pictorial, and symbolic.

Combining

Two-colored counters work well when they are used to show combinations of a particular quantity. For instance, children take a small handful of counters and place them on a surface. They can then record the number of red counters, yellow counters, and the total. They continue the activity in much the same way over and over to get a variety of combinations. They keep careful records of their work. Depending on the number of counters, they will end up with lists of combinations. Doing combinations encourages children to:
• count
• use addition when they do not realize that the total remains the same
• use subtraction as they realize that the total remains the same
• organize their answers in a list, as they realize that some combinations are missing (if they are).

Writing and Sharing

At first, combinations can be shown pictorially, but as the children's understanding grows, different levels of symbolic notation can be introduced. For instance, their recordings might look something like this.

An important question to ask during sharing is, "Are there any combinations we haven't got?" This encourages children to organize information as they do the experiments.

One way of organizing is by tables and charts. As children become accustomed to doing activities such as these, they will record the number of yellow and red pieces, rather than drawing pictures of the counters.

When the children are ready, help them connect these combinations to addition and subtraction facts. This might be done best by modeling addition facts first and following up with related subtraction facts. These types of connections bring the children to a symbolic level with smaller numbers. They then can use these facts when representing larger numbers.

Red	Yellow
● ● ●	○ ○ ○ ○ ○
● ● ● ●	○ ○ ○ ○

Red	Yellow
● ● ●	○ ○ ○ ○ ○
● ● ● ●	○ ○ ○ ○

$3 + 5 = 8$

$4 + 4 = 8$

Probability

Children often know expressions such as "a 50-50 chance," but do not really know what that means. Before introducing any kind of probability experiment, talk with the class about the 2 sides of a counter. Have children make predictions by asking, "Which side do you think will come up when it is tossed?" After the toss, talk with the children about the answer to this question: "If we toss a counter 10 times, how many times would red come up?"

Spend some time discussing vocabulary such as *likely, not likely, if...then, always,* and *never.*

Writing and Sharing

When using manipulatives, it is important for children to record their work. In fact, before children actually toss counters, they may prepare their recording page this way: Using red and yellow crayons, they can draw a number of empty circles. As they actually do the tosses, children fill in each circle with the appropriate color.

As they report the experiment, ask, "Which color came up more often?" If children have not organized their experiment into columns—horizontally or vertically—they must count to get the

MANAGEMENT TIP
Have children use pieces of construction paper as place mats onto which to spill their counters. This helps to prevent counters from falling on the floor.

answer. Through experience, they will begin to organize the information in some form of table or chart. The tables might look something like this:

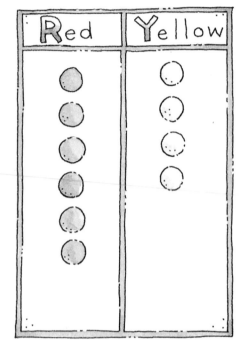
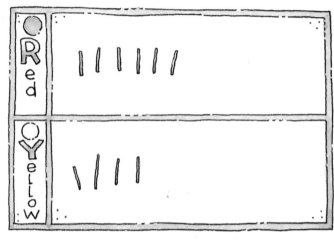

Organizing the record-keeping encourages children to use more symbolic representations, such as tallies.

A step toward the symbolic is showing the relationship between two occurrences. Model this for the class. After a demonstration toss, point out, for example, that there were 8 yellow out of 20 tries as well as 12 red out of 20 tries. Since these numbers do not show a perfect 1/2 and 1/2 distribution, it is important to talk about the relationship between the numbers.

Estimation is an important tool when talking about number relationships. As children become more sophisticated in their area, they will become more adept at determining approximate probability. For instance, numbers such as 8/20 and 12/20 will help children estimate that the experiment was *almost* 1/2 and 1/2.

Storing Two-Colored Counters

If the counters are to be used for counting, addition, and subtraction, store them in a sturdy, labeled, plastic bowl with a large opening. It is important for children to be able to reach into the bowl easily to take handfuls of counters.

A supply of 500 to 1,000 counters is usually sufficient for a class of approximately 30 children. Since children should be working in pairs, they will have an ample supply of counters regardless of the activity that they are involved in.

If the counters are to be used for combination activities, store the number of counters needed for each activity in small plastic bags that zip closed (such as a sandwich bag). Encourage children to count the materials before and after the lesson. Are the numbers the same? If children discover that they have been working with one or two less counters than they assumed, they have a reason to check their results. Overall, counting remains an important activity all through the primary grades.

Activities with Two-Colored Counters

Showing Combinations

Purpose: Randomly construct basic facts

Grouping of Students: Pairs

Materials: 10 counters in a plastic lunch bag for each pair, paper for recording

NCTM Standards: Mathematics as Problem Solving, Mathematics as Communication, Number Sense and Numeration, Whole Number Computation, Statistics and Probability

Directions:

1. Invite children to estimate how many counters they have in their bags. Have them record their estimates before they count.

2. Ask children to pick up their counters, gently shake them in the bags or in their hands, and spill them onto the desks.

3. Ask them to record the number of red and yellow counters for each toss. Continue tossing and recording outcomes for 15 to 20 minutes. Have children take turns spilling the counters on the desks and recording the results.

4. Encourage children to share the different combinations they got and their methods of counting. Record the combinations on the chalkboard or on a large piece of butcher paper.

5. After a substantial list has been created, ask, "What can we say about the different combinations?" Some children might find that 6 red and 4 yellow are "the same as" 4 red and 6 yellow. That is, the numbers are the same but the colors are different. Have the children look for other pairs. Some children will find the double 5 + 5.

6. Then ask the children if they think they have all the combinations possible. Chances are that combinations such as 10 + 0, 0 + 10, 1 + 9, and 9 + 1 did not occur. Encourage the class to create an organized list to see which, if any, combinations are missing.

7. You might want to keep this activity going throughout the school year. As children are comfortable with one total, such as 10, increase the total by 1 or 2 more counters. Encourage the children to keep ongoing records of their different totals.

8. Some volunteers will enjoy starting a booklet entitled "My Number Combinations." This activity will help children generate all possible basic facts in addition.

Assessment

As you observe children doing the activity, you will find that youngsters are on different conceptual levels. Some children will count the counters in each group and record the outcomes, either pictorially or symbolically, with numbers. Some children will count either the red or the yellow groups of counters and subtract the number from the total number. As children grapple with whether they have all possible combinations, some will look at what they have done and try to figure out what, if anything, is missing. They do not have a specific strategy to eliminate combinations. Others will look at their recordings and concentrate especially on combinations with larger numbers, such as 7 and 3, 8 and 2, and 9 and 1. Then they'll look at what they have and what is missing. Still others will study their recordings and approach them systematically. They'll focus on the combinations starting with 1, 2, 3, and so forth.

Probability

Purpose: Explore the probability of a two-colored counter showing one color or the other and recording the outcomes using a bar graph.

Grouping of Students: Pairs

Materials: Two-colored counter, paper for recording

NCTM Standards: Mathematics as Problem Solving, Mathematics as Communication, Number Sense and Numeration, Probability and Statistics

Directions:

1. Have the children fold the paper in half lengthwise and write the numbers 1-20 on each half vertically. Ask them to write RED on top of column 1 and YELLOW on the top of column 2.

2. Show the children a counter. Which color do they think will come up when the counter is tossed? Flip the counter a few times. Ask them to record each occurrence on their own sheets.

3. Have the children toss the counter about 20 times, each time recording the color that comes up.

4. How many times did children get yellow? red?

5. Distribute sheets of 1" square paper and have each pair color as many squares red as they had counters come up red. Do the same for yellow.

6. Have all the children in the class glue their red squares first and then

Red	Yellow
1. |	1.
2. |	2.
3.	3. |
4.	4. |
5. |	5.
6.	6. |
7. |	7.
8.	8.
9.	9.
10.	10.
11.	11.
12.	12.
13.	13.
14.	14.
15.	15.
16.	16.
17.	17.
18.	18.
19.	19.
20.	20.

their yellow squares on a large piece of butcher paper. This will create a graph, one bar showing red and the other bar showing yellow.

7. Have the children compare the 2 bars. Which color came up more frequently? (The 2 bars should be fairly even.)

8. Ask the children what they think would happen if they now tossed a counter. Have the children explain their answers.

Assessment

As children toss the counters, ask them about their predictions. Some boys and girls will predict that the color they like will come up. Others will say that every second time the yellow color will come up and every second time the counter will show red. Most children believe that if one color has come up 2 or 3 times in a row, the following flip will definitely show the other color. When children deal with 50/50 chance such as coins or two-color counters, they frequently believe that the sides take turns. First, for instance, yellow comes up, then the next turn will definitely be red.

Since a class of about 30 children will have tossed a counter approximately 300 times altogether, the graph they create will have close to a 50-50 distribution. As you observe the children interpreting the class graph, you'll notice that some children will still predict that tossing a counter would come up showing their favorite color. Some children will interpret the graph in such a way that the shorter bar will show the color the counter will show. This is because they believe that the bars should be even and it is the other column's turn. Others will predict that the taller bar shows the color that is the most likely to come up.

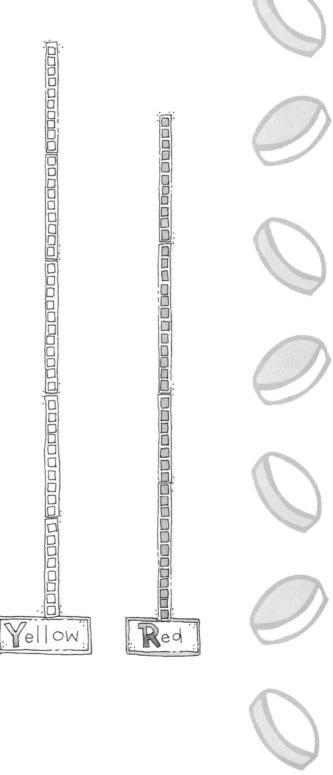

27

Plastic Links or Lots of Links

Links are useful for a variety of activities: patterning, measuring, sorting ("Put all the red links on the side of your desk"), counting, and grouping. Available in a variety of brilliant colors, links are especially appealing to young children.

Patterns

In their everyday lives, children observe a variety of patterns and designs. A pattern on a piece of clothing might follow an ABABAB pattern, but what we colloquially call a pattern might actually be a design. Children do not necessarily distinguish between patterns and designs. This is fine when it comes to everyday objects. However, when children begin to create their own mathematical patterns, it is important that they realize that each pattern has a rule that repeats. Consequently, when the rule is known (rule: ABABAB) as well as the components of the pattern (A= red, B=blue), the pattern can always be recreated.

Many manipulatives can be used for patterning activities, but children like links

because with them they can make ornaments they can wear, including necklaces, bracelets, and belts. Both boys and girls in kindergarten and first grade like using links for patterns and wearing their creations for all, or part of, the day.

Skip Counting Using Patterns

As children make their patterns, they should be encouraged to copy the pattern and color it. They should also tell about the pattern rule and how many times it repeats. As children learn the word names of the numbers and have a solid one-to-one counting correspondence, they can begin grappling with other ways to count. Patterns are conducive to skip counting, especially when the pattern rule is an obvious one, such as red, blue, red, blue. Encourage them to touch the last component of the pattern as they count.

Children frequently know how to skip count orally, even if they have little understanding of the underlying concept.

The concept can be introduced toward the end of kindergarten or the beginning of first grade. Initially, the numbers should be kept fairly small, about 10. Activities involving skip counting can be done by separating the links into groups of 2s. Have the children first count the links by 1s to be sure of how many there are. The children can then do the same activity by saying the odd numbers quietly and the even numbers louder. This way the children realize that when skip counting, the quantity still remains the same, whether they counted by 1s or by skip counting.

As the numbers become larger, the counting by 1s, using soft and loud voices, needs to be repeated many times. For example, if the quantity changes to 20, the children will need to go through the skip counting routine again. Each time the children should have an opportunity to compare the total they get when they skip count to the total when they count by 1s. Skip counting will later lead into multiplication.

Measuring

Links lend themselves well to measuring activities. They are flexible when combined and do not break apart easily. Links establish a standardized unit (one link). They are better to use than other flexible measuring tools, such as pieces of yarn or string.

When combined, links are longer and less rigid than snap cubes. They are also easier for young children to hold.

As usual, working in pairs will make the measuring easier than working individually.

MANAGEMENT TIP
Before an activity, model for the class how to use the links to measure smaller objects. Make exaggerated mistakes and wait for the children's reactions. For example, when measuring a pencil, place the first link in the middle. Add links until the tip of the pencil is reached. Announce your result, such as "My new pencil is two links long." Observe the responses from the children. These might include, "No it's longer!" or "You didn't measure this part." Encourage the children to tell, in their own words, how measuring should be done. Then remeasure the object, following the children's directions.

Child A can hold on to one end of the link chain as well as the object, while Child B can count or estimate the link-length of the object ("It's three links long!").

Writing and Sharing

After each activity, children should record what they measured and the lengths of the objects. Drawing pictures of the objects frees children from worrying about how to spell the objects' names. For those who want to write words, you can list the objects on the chalkboard.

Recording their findings will help children when comparing their measurements with those of other groups.

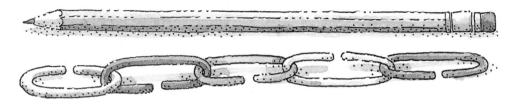

Storing the Links

Links can be stored in a plastic container with a large opening. An inexpensive painter's bucket is ideal because it is only about 10 inches high, can be carried easily, and fits well on a shelf. A shoe box also makes a good storage container. Label the containers for easy reference by you and the children.

When an activity calls for a specific number of links, the children can be asked to count out that number of links for themselves or for their classmates. The specific number of links can also be placed in individual plastic lunch bags before the lesson.

Activities with Links

Making Patterns

Purpose: Create patterns using color; use patterns to skip count
Grouping of Students: Individual
Materials: Links in different colors
NCTM Standards: Mathematics as Reasoning, Mathematical Connections, Patterns and Relationships
Directions:
1. If children do not know what patterns in mathematics are, show them a simple two-colored pattern. For example, red, blue, red, blue, red, blue. Ask children what color they think will come next. Repeat this activity a few times.
2. When children feel comfortable constructing patterns, have each child take a few handfuls of links or prepare bags ahead of time. Encourage the children to make patterns with their materials. Ask them to describe what part of the pattern repeats. Tell them that this part is called the pattern rule.

3. Ask children how they can use the pattern rule to help them count. If the children have constructed an AB pattern, they might suggest skip counting by 2. Have the children record underneath their pictures how they counted. Encourage them to include the total number of links used.

4. Ask the children to share their link patterns with the rest of the class. Have them tell how many links they used, how they counted, and what their pattern rules are. Encourage the children to ask questions about the patterns or comment about the patterns they see.

5. When children become comfortable with using an AB pattern, ask them to make more complex patterns. You might want to model different patterns that are variations of the basic AB pattern. For example, variations such as AAB, ABB, AABB are well within the reach of most young children.

6. Display children's patterns for the class to observe and copy. The links can be hung from hangers or strings.

Assessment

Most children will be successful using simple patterns. Some children, however, will be more interested in making very long chains using the links in front of them.

Some children will make patterns that reverse halfway through. For example, they start out making an AB pattern but reverse the pattern to a BA pattern. This is mainly because they are creating a symmetrical necklace or bracelet or this type of patterning satisfies them aesthetically. Ask the children to tell you about their pattern and how this pattern is the same or different from the one you modeled. Some children will 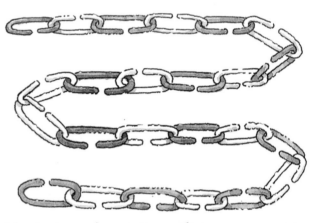 leave the simple patterns early on and begin to explore patterns that cover an area, rather than staying with a linear pattern.

Measuring

Purpose: Measure using links as standard units
Grouping of Students: Pairs
Materials: Links
NCTM Standards: Mathematics as Communication, Mathematics as Reasoning, Measurement
Directions:

1. Using links, have children measure objects in their desks. Ask children to record what they have measured. Boys and girls might draw pictures and write the length next to each illustration.

2. Have the children share and compare their work.

3. Then talk about how children think the results could be displayed. If they decide on sorting the items, they'll need to agree on a sorting rule, such as small, medium, and large objects.

4. Displaying the items might also be done as a bar or pictograph. Graphs lend themselves best to showing how many items have the same lengths. If pictographs are used, then the pictures of the items can be included in the bar and children can compare all the different objects with the same lengths.

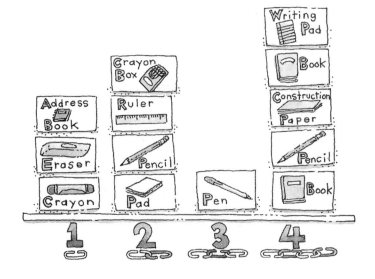

5. Continue by asking children to measure larger items in the classroom.

6. Have the pairs decide how many links they will put together to measure the different items. How will they count their measurements? Will 5 to 10 links put together be counted as one chain?

7. Have the children record what they measured and its length.

8. Again, invite children to display their results.

9. As time goes on, give youngsters opportunities to estimate how many links a particular object might be. In the beginning, stay with estimates such as "more than 10" or "less than 10" links. Later, have children estimate numerically (example: a pencil is about 3 links)

Assessment

You will note that some children will not align their measurement tool with the object being measured. Some children will have difficulty with the iteration of the unit they are using. For instance, every time they need to move the measurement tool, they will approximate where the previous one ended and where they need to put down the unit again. Some children, on the other hand, will measure by aligning and iterating the measurement tool without difficulty.

MANAGEMENT TIP
Since children need to move around the room freely, you might want to assign them specific classroom objects to measure and an order in which to do so. For example, the class as a whole might set up a list like this: chalkboard, door, teacher's desk, bookshelves, window length. The groups start at different points and work according to the list. (Group A starts with the chalkboard, while Group B starts with the bookshelves. When Group B reaches the bottom of the list, they resume at the top).

Addition and Subtraction

Purpose: Use three or more addends

Grouping of Students: Pairs

Materials: 20 + links in a plastic sandwich bag

NCTM Standards: Mathematics as Problem Solving, Mathematics as Reasoning, Mathematical Connections, Number Sense and Numeration, Whole Number Computation, Concepts of Whole Number Operations

Directions:

1. Invite each pair to estimate how many links are in their bag. Then ask children to count the links and compare the actual numbers to their estimates.

2. Have the children sort the links by color.

3. Ask the children how they can show 8 using 3 different colors. Have the children record their representations using numbers.

4. Have children use three or more colors to show 12, 15, 21 in as many ways as possible. Share representations.

5. Have children explore as many number representations as time permits, using 3 or more addends.

Assessment

As children explore representations of different numbers, some will approach the activity without using any particular strategies. They might count a few of one color, then add more of the second color, and finally, complete the representation with the last color. Sometimes they will use the same number combinations over and over, although the colors change. Some children will decide what numbers to use with the first 2 colors and count on with the third color. Others will start out with 3 even groups. They will then alter the groups, one at a time.

When children record their explorations, some boys and girls will record pictorially. Others will include numbers and words such as *and*, *is*, *make*, with their pictures. Still others will include number sentences with their drawings.

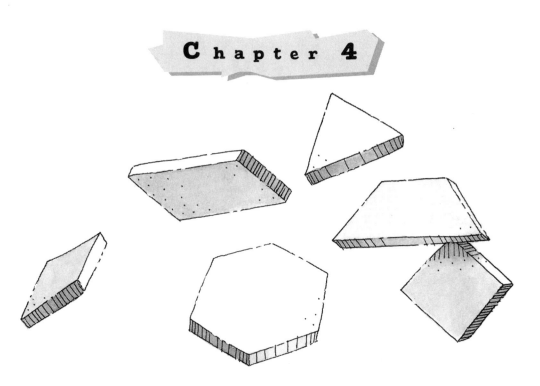

Pattern Blocks

As the name implies, pattern blocks are great for creating patterns and designs. Children like to put the pieces together to form designs. They use them almost like puzzle pieces.

As is true with many manipulatives, it is important to give children ample time to play with pattern blocks before beginning any pattern activity. Encourage children to create pictures using the shapes and then copy the pictures onto paper. While children work, you might want to introduce or review the names of the different shapes and relate these to shapes children see in their surroundings.

Names of Two-Dimensional Shapes
At the beginning of each lesson, gather the children around for short discussions of the names of the shapes. Introduce one shape at a time. Starting with the square, for example, ask the children where they have seen this shape before. Where do they see this shape in the classroom? What does this shape remind them of?

You might want to create lists of the shapes as they are introduced to the class. Use a large piece of paper, such as an experience chart or a piece of butcher paper. Be sure to include the name of each shape and a picture of it. Post the lists around the classroom, so the children can refer to them later as they construct and write about their work. Encourage children to look for these shapes in their neighborhoods. As months go by and children become aware of different shapes, they may add new names and pictures, even after the pattern blocks activity has been completed.

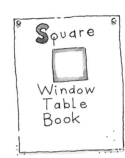

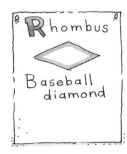

Creating Linear Patterns

When children are ready to do specific activities involving patterns, introduce a simple pattern such as the following:

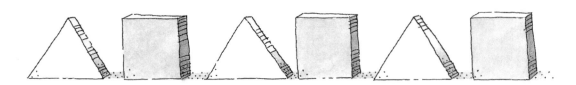

When introducing a pattern activity, put out each pattern block, one at a time. After putting out the last square, ask the children if they can figure out what might come next. As children suggest a triangle, ask if everybody agrees with the suggestion and to explain their reasoning. The children will tell about what they see without necessarily separating the triangle and square as the pattern that repeats over and over. Have the children spend some time creating patterns of their own and recording and sharing these patterns.

Repeat the whole group activity many times, introducing more complicated patterns as the class is ready. After the different combinations with 2 shapes have been exhausted, introduce a third shape, such as a trapezoid. The pattern might look something like this: ABCABC. As children become accustomed to dealing with patterns, introduce vocabulary such as *repeating patterns* and *pattern rule.*

Creating Area Patterns

As children explore patterns, they begin to create more intricate ones but usually stay with linear patterns such as those in the examples above. Introduce the children to area patterns by modeling a pattern that repeats, not only horizontally but also vertically, as shown here.

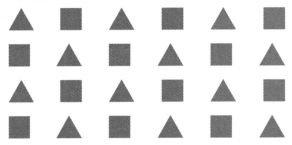

36

Be sure the pattern repeats fully, twice, to give children a chance to identify the pattern rule.

Have the children talk about what is different about an area-pattern setup compared with a linear one. At first, the children might concentrate on one row at a time, paying little attention to the columns. If so, focus their attention on the first column, then on the second, and so forth. Have the children play around with this type of pattern for a while, then ask them if they can think of any others.

Sometimes young children want to stay on a level at which they feel comfortable and may not want to venture any further. As they continue to create patterns throughout the primary grades, though, they will become more and more inventive with their work.

Writing and Sharing

As children record their patterns, encourage them to include in their drawing the part of the pattern that repeats. As they tell about their patterns, ask them to name the shapes they used. Sometimes children mix up the names for the shapes. If that happens, simply restate the entire sentence the children used, but use the proper terminology for the shapes.

In their recordings most young children use pictures when describing geometric shapes. By second grade many children want to use their writing skills and begin to write the names of the shapes together with their drawings. The shape lists, created earlier, will alleviate time-consuming struggles with spelling.

Figuring Out Area and Perimeter

Pattern blocks can also be used to informally figure out area and perimeter. Children use pattern blocks to cover an area and count how many blocks it takes to cover that space. Depending on what the children want to cover, the square pattern block might be the easiest shape to start with, but triangles, trapezoids, and hexagons will also work. In most cases, some of the area will not be covered completely, regardless of which pattern blocks are used.

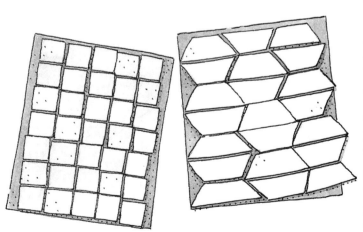

The children should be encouraged to estimate how many more of that pattern block it would take to cover the empty spots. Encourage children to use the word *about* in their recordings after they have estimated the area of any one shape.

Have children cover each shape twice, each time with different pattern blocks. For instance, if they first covered their shapes with squares, ask them to cover the shape the second time with a trapezoid or hexagon.

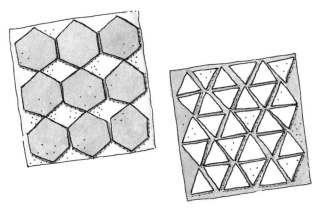

Writing and Sharing

Encourage the children to record each outcome. As they share their findings, ask children what they noticed when they covered their shapes first with squares and then with hexagons. The more frequently the children do activities such as these, the more aware they become of the relationship between the size of the pattern block and the number of pattern blocks needed to cover an area. That is, the larger the pattern block the fewer the shapes needed to cover the area.

Generalizing About the Size and Number of Units

The relationship between the size of unit and the number of units needed to cover an area is an important one for children to internalize. This relationship exists whenever the children measure anything. Some children will have enough everyday experiences to find this relationship a natural one. Other children might need time to explore a variety of measurements before they are ready to generalize.

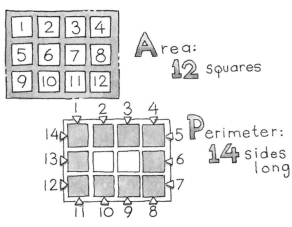

Just as children count the shapes it takes to cover a surface, they also count the number of sides it takes to make up the perimeter. When talking about the perimeter, it is better if children use shapes such as triangles and squares. (The trapezoid and hexagon do not work very well for perimeter.) The children have difficulty when counting how many units make up the perimeter, because they have a tendency to count shapes rather than the sides of the shape. Children feel that they can only count one side of a shape and usually omit the second side of the corner shapes.

Fractions

Pattern blocks can be used to introduce or reinforce the concept of equal parts and fractions. Colloquially, fraction names are frequently used when describing approximate parts of a whole. It is important that children realize that 1/2 of a whole is 1 of 2 equal parts that make up the whole. (Using food to model fractions of a whole is almost an impossible activity. There is always a bigger and smaller part.) Using pattern blocks to show fractions, though, is most helpful. Children can use the different pattern blocks to see how many smaller blocks cover a larger pattern block. For example:

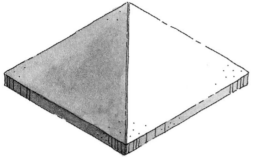
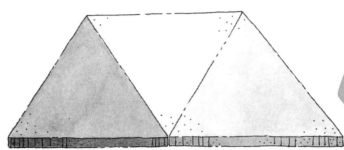

Writing and Sharing

Have the children explore the different combinations of pattern blocks that fully cover larger shapes. Ask them to record their findings and to share these with classmates. When children record their findings, encourage them to trace the smaller pattern blocks in the configuration that makes up the larger shape. When children draw these shapes free-hand, they lose the important aspect of equal parts.

Storing Pattern Blocks

Pattern blocks can be stored in a variety of containers, such as small buckets, shoe boxes, or large plastic food containers. The labeled container must have a large opening, of course, to make it easy for children to help themselves to the materials. If cardboard shoe boxes are used, cover them with a self-adhesive plastic covering. The boxes last longer and are sturdier.

If possible, invest in plastic shoe boxes. Plastic containers are more rigid than cardboard boxes and therefore easier to carry. Paint stores have a variety of inexpensive, semidisposable buckets that also work very well.

MANAGEMENT TIP

If room for storage is a problem, use shoe box containers. If storage space is adequate, use a variety of different-shaped containers. They add texture to the classroom and give children a variety of shapes to discuss.

Activities with Pattern Blocks

Using Pattern Blocks to Give Directions

Purpose: Give directions and visualize two-dimensional shapes and how they fit together.

Grouping of Students: Pairs

Materials: A handful of assorted pattern blocks, book or divider for each pair

NCTM Standards: Mathematics as Problem Solving, Mathematics as Communication, Geometry and Spatial Sense

Directions:

1. Invite each pair to take an assortment of pattern blocks, but no more than 5 pieces.

2. Explain that it is important that the children work together. The pair is finished when both partners are done. Set up a book or divider between the partners.

3. In the beginning, suggest that children use no more than 2 to 5 pattern blocks. Ask Partner A to use the pattern blocks to make a design and to tell Partner B about the design. Partner B is to recreate the design using his or her materials. Partner B is not allowed to ask clarifying directions but must follow directions as best he/she can.

4. When finished, have children compare designs. How close did Partner B get?

5. Have the partners switch the roles and repeat the activity.

Assessment

Observe how well children give directions that are easy to follow and how well they follow directions. Children should also work cooperatively with each other.

Some children will make appropriate designs. They will, however, find giving directions difficult and will also repeat some directions. This will lead to misunderstandings by their partners.

Other children will make simple designs but lack directional words or misunderstand directional words.

Still others will make simple designs and communicate or interpret the directions correctly.

Tessellating or Tiling

Purpose: Cover the plane with one or two pattern blocks, generalizing about the relationship between size and number. (The larger the shape, the fewer pattern blocks needed.)

Grouping of Students: Individual

Materials: For each child, a sandwich bag filled with pattern blocks. Include at least 3 different types of pattern blocks, enough of each shape to cover the square piece of paper. For each child, several sheets of 3"x 3" paper.

NCTM Standards: Mathematics as Problem Solving, Mathematics as Communication, Mathematics as Reasoning, Geometry and Spatial Sense, Patterns and Relationships

Directions:

1. Distribute materials.

2. Model what it means to tessellate or tile the piece of paper using pattern blocks.

3. Give children time to play with their pattern blocks and to cover the paper with the materials. Ask children to copy their tiling onto paper.

4. Invite children to use only 1 of their shapes and to cover the square with that shape. Ask them to draw their work and to write the number of pattern blocks they used.

5. Now ask children to use another shape and do the same activity.

6. Have children compare the number of smaller shapes needed with the number of larger shapes needed.

7. Have children use different shapes and tile the paper using a repeating pattern. Ask them to copy their tiling and to share the pattern they made.

Assessment

Observe how children approach the tiling task. Also observe how they respond to your question about comparing shapes.

Some children will not make a comparison, but report the two sets of numbers. Others will compare the numbers and shapes but not make a generalization. For instance, it

takes more triangles than trapezoids to cover the paper. Still other children will generalize, stating that when the shape is big, it only takes a few pattern blocks to cover it. When the shape is smaller, it takes more pattern blocks to cover the paper.

When asked to use all their shapes to tile the paper, some children will tile without creating a pattern. Others will create a pattern but will repeat it horizontally, not vertically. They will create a new pattern for each row. Still others will use the same pattern, repeating the pattern both horizontally and vertically.

Creating Fractional Relationships

Purpose: Use pattern blocks to partition a whole into equal parts
Grouping of Students: Individual or pairs
Materials: An assortment of pattern blocks, paper for recording
NCTM Standards: Mathematics as Problem Solving, Mathematics as Communication, Geometry and Spatial Sense, Fractions and Decimals, Patterns and Relationships
Directions:
1. Have each child take a handful of pattern blocks.
2. Ask the children how many red trapezoids it would take to cover a yellow hexagon. Share responses.
3. Ask the children to explore if there are any other shapes that completely cover the surface of another shape. Have them record their answers. In order to recreate the fractional parts of a whole, suggest that children trace the smaller shapes that make up the larger whole.
4. Ask: "Do you know what each part is called when a whole is divided into 2 equal parts? 3 equal parts? 4 equal parts? Introduce the vocabulary *half, third,* and *fourth*, if children do not suggest it.
5. Ask children to compare 1/3 of a hexagon (blue rhombus) with 1/3 of a trapezoid (green triangle). Both are called 1/3, but they are not the same size. What makes the difference?

Assessment

Observe if children see that the size of the whole determines the size of the fraction.

Some youngsters will see that a rhombus is larger than a triangle, but they will deal with each shape as a whole, not as a fractional part.

Other youngsters will agree that both shapes are a part of a set of 3 when covering a larger shape. They will not relate to each being 1/3 of something but will agree that 1 shape is larger than the other.

Still other youngsters will see that both pieces represent 1/3 of larger shapes. The larger 1/3 came from the set that covered the larger shape, the smaller 1/3 came from the set that covered the smaller shape.

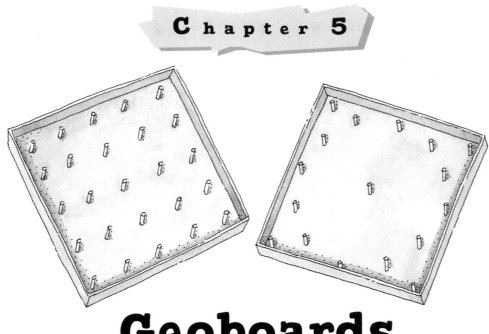

Geoboards

Children find geoboards fun and use them to make a variety of designs. Geoboards come in different sizes. Young children work better on the geoboards that are 6 inches or larger.

Before they get started, talk with the class about acceptable behavior for using the materials. Some of the rules that prevent children from getting hurt follow:
  • Both hands must hold on to the rubber band when placing it on the pegs of the geoboard.
  • Place the rubber band around one peg first and then stretch it gently to the other pegs.
  • When taking the rubber bands off, remove the band from one peg first, and then from the others.

Writing and Sharing
Children need ample time to explore creating a variety of designs before being asked to copy or record two-dimensional shapes. In some cases, the designs that children create are too intricate for them to copy.

After the children have had time to explore, encourage them to create two-dimensional shapes and to copy their shapes on blank paper. This activity encourages children to count the pegs on a geoboard, to create an area with a given number of square units, and to use their spatial visualization skills when approximating the distances between pegs.

Let children create their own dot paper before drawing shapes.

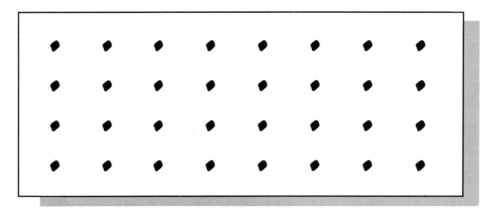

(Commercial dot paper is available, but it is often no easier to use than that created by the children themselves. Using commercially created dot paper removes some of the richness of children's recording of their geoboard activities.)

Geoboard Fractions

Children can easily divide shapes into parts using the geoboard. These parts might not be equal in size and might vary greatly in size and shape. Encourage children to talk about the smaller shapes contained in the larger shape.

This is a good way to have children talk about geometric properties, geometric vocabulary, and compound shapes.

Have children record the smaller shapes contained within the larger shapes. Ask children if the the smaller shapes are the same size.

After awhile, construct activities that encourage children to divide the larger shapes into equal parts, such as 1/2s, 1/3s, and 1/4s. Ask the children to tell how many parts they have and why these parts are the same size. Encourage the children to connect the number of parts with the name of the fractions. Of course, there is no reasonable connection between 2 and halves, but 3 and thirds becomes easier and 4 and fourths already make sense. Children have used the terms *third* and *fourth* when dealing with ordinal numbers, but the connection is elusive.

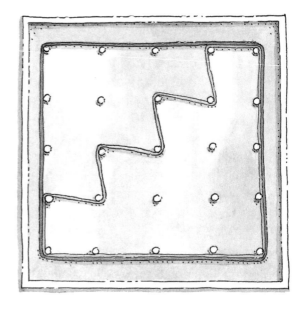

At first, children will divide the geoboard shapes symmetrically and visually determine that the shapes are of equal size. Later, children will explore other ways to divide the shapes. Usually, they divide the shapes in staircase fashion. This type of exploration will lead them into counting whole squares formed by the pegs on the geoboard.

Determining Areas of Shapes

Encourage children to compare the sizes of the shapes they made with the sizes of the shapes made by their partners. Ask children to determine whose shape covers more space and to explain how they determined the areas of the shapes.

Writing and Sharing

Children will try to decide how many squares each shape covers. The shapes they create usually include some whole geoboard squares. Children will first count these whole squares. Then they will combine the partial squares until they feel that they have the area of a whole square. At the end, the children add all the squares they have counted. After the children have compared the area of a variety of shapes, ask them to draw some shapes in their math journals and to write about how they decided which shape was larger.

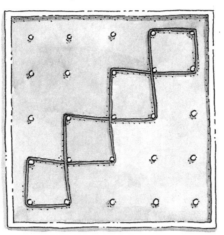

Determining Perimeters of Shapes

After children make squares or rectangles on their geoboards and figure out the areas of these shapes, encourage them to then tell the perimeter of the shapes.

Geometric Vocabulary

As children use geoboards to create two-dimensional shapes, introduce relevant vocabulary.

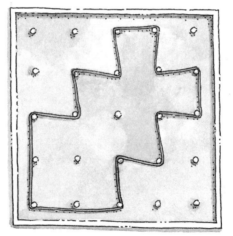

Most children will talk about the *corners* of a shape, rather than the *vertex* or *vertices*. This is fine for young children, but they should also be introduced to the correct term.

For example, ask the children to describe a shape. Repeat what the children have described. As you mention the number of "corners," you might say, "Another name for *corner* is *vertex*. If you have many corners, you call them *vertices*." Then continue with the description.

This approach can be used with all the geometric vocabulary, introducing *edge* (for "side") and *angle* ("for straight corners").

By making connections between children's everyday language and geometric terminology, all children have an opportunity to be included in the learning process. It empowers children to make the connections between known words and concepts and new ones.

Storing Geoboards

Geoboards can be stacked on a tray that has a small edge. The tray makes it easy to transport the geoboards and keeps them contained within that space. Do not stack the geoboards too high, or they will fall off as the tray is carried. Some disposable aluminum roasting pans are large enough to hold quite a few geoboards and might be preferable to trays.

Depending on the size and number of geoboards, consider storing some in a drawstring cloth bag. Cloth drawstring bags are easily made from pillow cases. They are also easy for children to carry. Even if the bag is knocked off the shelf, the geoboards will not scatter. The only drawback to a bag is that the manipulatives are not visible on the shelf.

Activities with Geoboards

Making Shapes

Purpose: Use geoboards to create simple and compound shapes
Grouping of Students: Individual
Materials: Geoboards and rubber bands, paper for recording
NCTM Standards: Mathematics as Problem Solving, Geometry and Spatial Sense
Directions:

1. Have children create simple geometric shapes.
2. Encourage the children to draw each shape and to write or tell about the shapes. For example, for a picture of a square, children might write or tell the name of the shape and add, "It has four sides and four straight corners."
3. Ask children to start out with one large, simple shape and then create small shapes within the large one.
4. Have children draw the shapes they made and write or tell about the shapes, including the geometric names of the shapes they know. Encourage them to include the shape they started out with.
5. Ask children to make a combination of shapes, such as a square and a triangle touching each other. How many different combinations of shapes can they make?
6. Have the children draw the combinations and write or tell about the two or more shapes they have made. What do the combinations remind them of?

46

Assessment

Some children will outline their geoboard shapes without recreating the geoboards themselves. They will use a combination of colloquial descriptive terms as they tell about their shapes. For example, when describing the trapezoid they will talk about the shape as having four sides and four corners and refer to it as being upside down. They will not necessarily include the geometric name of the shape, such as a trapezoid.

Other children will recreate the geoboard using dots, then draw the shape connecting the dots. Because the dots are not evenly distributed, the shape will not be a copy of the geoboard shape. The biggest discrepancy will show in the angles. Children will describe their shapes using colloquial terms and include the geometric name of the shape.

Still other children will begin by copying the shape, getting a fairly good likeness. They will then put in the dots to show the placement of the geoboard pegs. When describing the shapes, the children will describe many detailed geometric properties. For instance, the children will describe two sides as being straight. This means the two parallel edges. They will also describe two of the angles as being "smaller" than straight corners (acute), and two angles as being "bigger" than straight corners (obtuse).

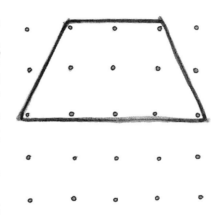

Making Pictures and Formulating Problems

Purpose: Create story problems using pictures children have made

Grouping of Students: Pairs

Materials: Geoboards, rubber bands, paper for recording

NCTM Standards: Mathematics as Problem Solving, Mathematics as Communication, Geometry and Spatial Sense

Directions:

1. Distribute materials.
2. Tell children to take turns making pictures using the geoboards.
3. Ask children to copy the pictures onto pieces of drawing paper.
4. Have children formulate problems using their pictures as a basis. Encourage them to use the different shapes in their pictures.
5. Ask children to include a question that will have numbers or shape names as answers to their problems.

Assessment

Children like telling stories and are usually quite successful telling about the work they have been doing. Since formulating mathematical problems has as its purpose an answer that can be deduced from the problem itself, formulating mathematical problems is a slow developmental process in children. They need to see the importance the questions serve.

As children work, you will notice that some tell a story about their pictures that will not necessitate a question. Others will include a question, but they have already answered the question or it might not have much to do with the problem. Still other children will enumerate shapes or representations they have created and ask a question that can be answered from their pictures.

Creating Symmetrical Shapes

Purpose: Use geoboards to explore symmetry
Grouping of Students: Pairs
Materials: Geoboards and rubber bands, paper for recording
NCTM Standards: Mathematics as Problem Solving, Mathematics as Communication, Geometry and Spatial Sense
Directions:
1. Have two children work together, taking turns.
2. Tell them that they are going to copy each other's shapes. The shapes need to touch one another. Model an example of 2 touching designs, where the line of symmetry divides the original shape from the copied shape.
3. Have one partner create a shape using half the geoboard.
4. Then have the other partner copy the shape as if she or he were using a mirror.
5. Ask the children to copy their shapes on paper, coloring one of their designs one color and the other design another color.
6. Have the children describe what they think would happen if they cut out the whole design and folded it where the two designs meet.
7. Tell the children that the folding line is called the *line of symmetry*.
8. Encourage the children to make more designs that could be folded so that both sides would be the same.

Assessment

You will find that some children make geometric designs that have one point, or vertex, touching. These might be triangles, diamonds, or trapezoids. Encourage the children to create designs that have an edge touching rather than only a vertex.

Other children will use an imaginary line dividing the geoboard and create geometric designs with an edge touching rather than a vertex. If the children put 2 triangles or 2 trapezoids together, encourage them to look at the whole shape. Ask them what shape two of these geometric shapes create together. Some children will create irregular shapes. Their shapes will not be as easy to copy as regular geometric shapes. Encourage the children to talk about the number of edges and vertices their shapes have. If possible, encourage them to name their shapes, such as hexagons, heptagons, or octagons.

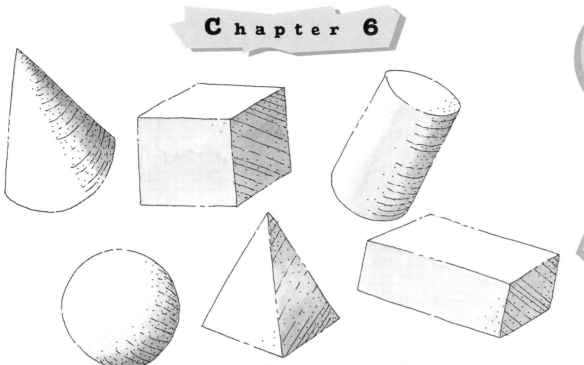

Geometric Solids or Geoblocks

A complete set of geometric solids includes many shapes that children in the primary grades do not need to explore. In the primary grades, children need to recognize the properties of at least 6 of them. These are the cone, the cube, the cylinder, the pyramid, the rectangular prism, and the sphere. Many of these shapes are known to children by their colloquial names. For instance, children usually call the cylinder a can, the rectangular prism a box, and the sphere a ball. Before beginning any organized activities that include the geometric solids, introduce these 6 shapes, one at a time, and have the children explore and describe the blocks.

Exploring Three-Dimensional Shapes

Begin the exploration with the more familiar objects, such as the cube, the rectangular prism, and the cylinder. After the children have spent some time exploring these shapes, give the children the rest of the shapes: the cone, the pyramid, and the sphere.

Set up shape lists as was done with the pattern blocks. Draw the individual shapes and write the shape names. Whenever the different shapes are discussed, keep a set of the geoblocks in front of the children and available for them to touch. Ask children what the shapes remind them of. Although the children early on are aware of the differences between two-dimensional shapes and three-dimensional shapes, they frequently use

the names for these shapes interchangeably. Sometimes this happens because of the children's vantage points. They see only one side of a three-dimensional shape. Sometimes they do not visualize the whole shape, and at times they forget what the three-dimensional shape is called.

Writing and Sharing

Encourage children to spend time exploring the shapes and recording things they can tell about the shapes. Young children usually do not draw in perspective but instead include every part of the shape they can possibly fit in. For instance, a cube will look as if it were seen from the side; the top as if it had been partially flattened as well as opened up.

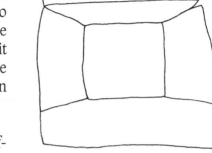

Encourage the children to write about the different shapes.

Properties of Three-Dimensional Shapes

As the children work, include activities that encourage them to pay attention to the properties or functions of the shapes. "Guess my shape" is always useful. In this game, one hides a shape behind the back, in a bag, or in a tube sock. The shape is out of view to the children who are to guess the shape from the description you provide.

Additional "Guess my shape" activity: You, or a volunteer, describe an object in the classroom. Children guess what the object is and bring it to the "leader."

Geometric Vocabulary

Be sure to use the correct geometric vocabulary as often as possible, including the names of geometric solids. When children talk about *cans*, insert *cylinder* during the discussion. As children describe something as a *box*, use *rectangular prism* or *cube* whenever possible. Since a ball is a *sphere*, use the correct term accordingly.

Building with Shapes

To create opportunities for children to build with three-dimensional shapes, ask parents to send to school any kind of empty packaging. (For example, cereal boxes, tissue boxes, oatmeal canisters, and hot cocoa canisters. In addition, small balls, cone-shaped objects, and pyramids or cubes will be helpful.)

Robot

Dog

7 shapes

Using the three-dimensional objects, have children create structures. Encourage youngsters to work in pairs. Children may need your help as they tape or glue the different shapes together.

50

Writing and Sharing

Ask the children to draw pictures of their shape creations in their math journals. If possible, they should also write descriptions of their work. Encourage the children to use as reference the pictures and vocabulary on the class lists. Invite children to include the number of shapes they used in all, the number of same (different) shapes they used. This might be an opportunity to graph the number of shapes used in each of the individual shape creations.

Storing the Geometric Solids

If you have only a dozen or so geometric solids, they can be stored in a large boxlike container. If, however, you have a large number of geometric solids, a bag might be more useful. Use a pillow case, a large net bag (such as the kind citrus fruits come in), or a laundry bag. Again, label the storage container with the individual shape names or with the words *Geometric Solids* or *Geoblocks*.

If you have only a few geometric solids, you might want the children to explore all the solids simultaneously: Each pair of children explores one solid at a time, but all the solids are used simultaneously. In that case, store all the geometric solids together in a large box or a bag.

If you have only a few geometric solids, consider placing them on a sturdy tray in a learning center. Children can explore them at their leisure.

MANAGEMENT TIP
As the solids are introduced to the class, it might be best to put on the shelf only the shape that is being introduced. You might want to keep these shapes in a large box or on a tray.

Activities with Geometric Solids

Shadow Pictures

Purpose: Distinguish the different faces of three-dimensional shapes
Grouping of Students: Whole class
Materials: An assortment of three-dimensional shapes and an overhead projector
NCTM Standards: Geometry and Spatial Sense, Mathematics as Communication, Mathematics as Problem Solving
Directions:
1. Tell the children that they are going to play a game with the different three-dimensional shapes or geoblocks.
2. During the lesson, encourage children to talk quietly with their neighbor about the shape they see on the screen. To which three-dimensional shape might it belong?
3. Place a shape, such as a cube, on the overhead projector. Tell the children that this is one face of the shape. What shape is it?
4. If children do not know, show them another face. Keep going until someone correctly identifies the shape.
5. Ask the child to tell the class how he or she decided that the shape must be a cube.
6. Continue with other shapes, such as a rectangular prism.
7. Allow volunteers to take over your role.

Assessing the Work Children Do

Allow the children to keep a set of geometric solids in front of them as the game is played. You will find that some children have not thought of a shape as having distinct parts. Encourage them to discuss with a partner what they see and to list all the different shapes that have faces like the one before them.

Some children find faces of cubes and rectangular prisms easy to identify but feel stumped when it comes to other three-dimensional shapes. Other youngsters find it less of a challenge.

Tracing Three-Dimensional Shapes

Purpose: Using geometric solids to explore the properties of three-dimensional shapes
Grouping of Students: Pairs
Materials: Rectangular prisms, cubes, cones, pyramids, cylinders, construction paper, and masking tape

NCTM Standards: Geometry and Spatial Sense, Mathematics as Communication, Mathematics as Problem Solving

Directions:

1. Have pairs of children choose a geoblock.

2. Invite each pair to trace on paper the faces of the solid and cut out the two-dimensional shapes.

3. Have the pairs record the shapes and describe each one.

4. Using masking tape, have children work together to recreate the shape.

5. Continue with other shapes.

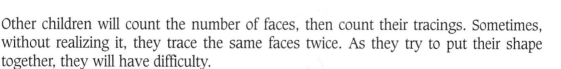

Assessment

As you observe the children tracing, you will find that some do so without regard to the number of faces on the three-dimensional shape. It will become obvious to them that they are missing faces as they put the shapes together. They will not always know what face is missing, as they go back to the original shape to trace missing ones. Their records might show the same confusion.

Other children will count the number of faces, then count their tracings. Sometimes, without realizing it, they trace the same faces twice. As they try to put their shape together, they will have difficulty.

Still other children use a marking system. They might apply pieces of masking tape to a face after it has been traced.

Trash Monsters

Purpose: To distinguish functional properties of three-dimensional shapes, such as empty packaging

Grouping of Students: Pairs

Materials: An assortment of everyday three-dimensional shapes

NCTM Standards: Geometry and Spatial Sense, Mathematics as Communication, Mathematics as Reasoning, Mathematics as Problem Solving

Directions:

1. Distribute an assortment of empty, everyday packaging.

2. Ask the children to create a monster with the shapes.

3. Have children draw what they created and describe the three-dimensional shapes they used.

4. Talk with the class about the placements of the shapes. Could they place any of the shapes on the bottom? In the middle? On top of their constructions?

5. Can children generalize about the functions the different shapes serve?

Assessment

You will find that some children build horizontally; that is, they build one block high. Others will stack only cubes or rectangular prisms as they create Trash Monsters. Still others will use a variety of shapes and a trial-and-error exploration to find out if the different shapes stack. Their monsters tend to be tall.

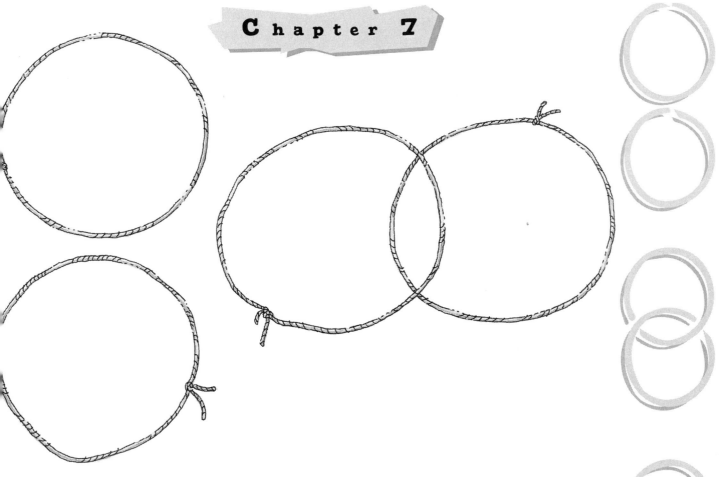

Venn Diagrams

In primary grades, Venn diagrams are often limited to 2 or 3 circles. (If circles intersect, two are challenging enough for young children. If circles are separate, the youngsters can handle three.)

If children are to work on the floor, start with about 2 or 3 yards of yarn. If they are to work on the tops of tables or desks, use 1 or 1 1/2 yards of yarn.

Sorting Using Circles

Sorting activities are an important part of geometry. Young children often look at geometric shapes as a whole, rather than focusing on the components and properties.

Children need to see a purpose for using Venn diagrams. They need to understand that objects and shapes can fit into 2 or more categories at one time. (For example, a ball can be round as well as green.)

In addition, children should be made aware that when using intersecting circles, they must not count the same items twice if computing the total number of items.

Separated or Disjoint Circles

Begin the sorting activities with 2 yarn circles that are disjointed, or clearly apart from each other.

Gather a variety of everyday classroom materials. How might these be sorted into 2 groups? Children usually focus on color, size, and shape. Children might suggest sorting the items into large or small objects. Sort the objects one at a time.

Children might disagree as to whether some objects are large or small. Ask youngsters to place those objects on the outside of the circles. Later, have the children make decisions for the remaining objects. At the end of the activity ask, "Is there another way to sort the objects?"

Intersecting Circles

As children sort objects into 2 distinct groups, they will find that some objects belong to both groups. (For example, where do they put a large green object if one circle is labeled Big, the other Green?)

In such a lesson, have children place the items in questions on the outside of the labeled circles. Where should the items go? Create an intersection with the yarn. Place the item in the space shared by both circles. You now have a Venn diagram with intersecting circles. Have children talk about what they see and how they interpret the 2 intersecting circles.

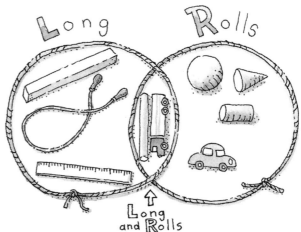

When you have done many sorting activities like these, ask how many items are in one circle and how many are in the other. Record the numbers. Sometimes the children want to count the items as belonging to both groups. If this happens, have the children compare their final number with the number of physical objects.

Writing and Sharing
Encourage the children to draw pictures of what they have done.

Storing Intersecting Circles
Commercially available plastic circles can be stored in a bag or on a large tray. Homemade yarn circles may be kept in a large plastic bag that zips closed.

Activities with Venn Diagrams

Sorting with Circles
Purpose: Choose attributes by which to sort
Materials: 2 sorting circles, a variety of classroom objects such as pattern blocks, attribute blocks, links, geometric solids, books, toys, and blocks
Grouping of Students: Whole class or large group
NCTM Standards: Mathematics as Problem Solving, Mathematics as Communication, Number Sense and Numeration, Statistics and Probability, Patterns and Relationships
Directions:
1. Prepare a set of cards with labels such as LARGE and SMALL, RED and BLUE, ROUND and SQUARE, LONG and SHORT. You can add other sets at a later time.
2. Lay out the 2 circles, providing ample space between them. Keep the objects apart from the circles.
3. Have children talk about how the items could be sorted. If children do not mention it themselves, suggest that they sort by size.
4. Place the label SMALL above one of the circles. Then place LARGE above the other circle.
5. Have the children sort one object at a time.
6. If an item does not belong in either circle (perhaps it is medium-sized), place it outside the circles.
7. When all items have been placed, have children estimate and compare the number of items in each circle and the

number of items outside the circles. About how many are in the first circle? In the second circle? Outside the circles?

8. Have children draw pictures of their work.

9. Ask children to write the actual numbers underneath each set. Have them compare their estimates to the actual numbers.

Assessment

Observe how children decide where each item belongs. Some children will decide the placement of the items according to an internal rule. For example, they might determine the size of an item based on whether or not it fits in their hands.

Other children will place borderline objects outside both circles rather than placing them in either one.

Still other children will make decisions based on items already placed. With this method, children place all items into one circle or the other.

Introducing Intersecting Circles

Purpose: Explore sorting by attribute; see that some objects might belong in two different groups

Materials: 2 sorting circles and a variety of three-dimensional objects such as geometric solids, boxes, cans, balls, toys from the classroom that fit into the category of three-dimensional shapes, blocks

Grouping of Students: Whole class or large group

NCTM Standards: Geometry and Spatial Sense, Mathematics as Problem Solving, Mathematics as Communication, Number

Sense and Numeration, Statistics and Probability, Patterns and Relationships

Directions:

1. Label sets of index cards STACKS and DOES NOT STACK, ROLLS and DOES NOT ROLL, RED and NOT RED.

2. Lay out 2 circles so that they are sufficiently far apart for a group of objects to fit between them.

3. Place the label STACKS above one of the circles. Place the label DOES NOT STACK above the other.

4. Have the children choose one object at a time and place it in either circle.

5. Ask youngsters to give their rationales.

6. Encourage other children to agree or disagree with the first player's decisions.

7. If the other children disagree (because it could be placed in either circle), place that object between the circles.

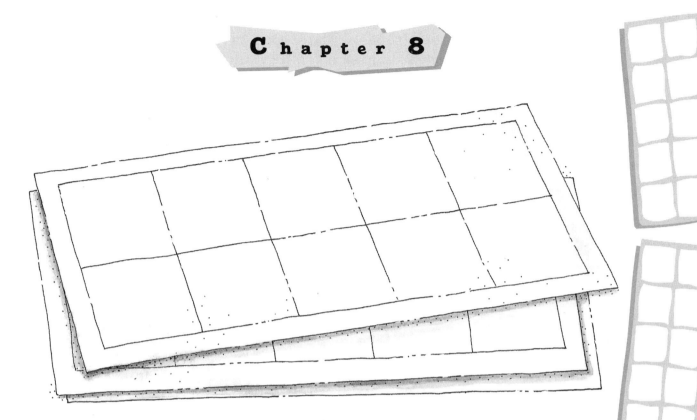

Tens Frames

To make 10s frames, draw on oaktag or large index cards and cover with clear contact paper. Make each side of each square 1 1/2 inches to 2 inches long. Be sure that the 10s frame has two rows of five cells. This will allow children to visualize the quantity of 5 before going on to 10.

Counting

In primary grades, counting remains one of the most important concepts to be developed. Children also need
• to learn the names of the numbers, as well as the number sequence
• to develop an understanding of one-to-one correspondence between objects and number words
• to develop a sense of relative magnitude of quantities.

Children also need to look at relationships within quantities. Different counting strategies, such as grouping, skip counting, and visualizing number patterns, help children develop this skill. In the beginning, children should explore counting and using strategies, but concrete manipulations must be connected to symbolic expressions.

Many children in kindergarten have a good knowledge of how to count by rote past 20. In first grade, they can rote count past 100, although the names for the number words get confused around the different decades. For instance, it is not unusual for children to count 38, 39, 30-10, 30-11, and so forth. In second grade, children can manage numbers in the hundreds. In most of these cases, children might find it difficult to count larger quantities using a one-to-one correspondence. Often the difficulty lies in the fact that the children do not know how to organize their counting.

Tens frames allow children to organize their counting into manageable chunks. The 10s frames help children with the quantity of objects by allowing them to concentrate on placing objects into squares. Once the frame is filled, they also know the size of the group. If they have an unlimited number of frames, the children can continue filling frames until they have exhausted all the items they want to count. If the children have only one frame, they can remove the objects

from the 10s frame into a group on the side until they have counted all their items. As long as the children keep the groups of 10 separated, their task does not have to be repeated. The final part of the counting task is to count the groups.

Here the efficiency lies in skip counting by 10s. In order for the children to do this, they need to know the sequence of numbers when counting by 10s. Developmentally, the children also need to understand cardinality. They must know that the last number said in a counting sequence tells the size of the quantity. The children also need to understand that skip counting by any number pertains only to the groups of that size. If there are some objects left uncounted after grouping by 10, they should be counting by 1, not 10.

Addition and Subtraction

In kindergarten and first grade, introduce these activities using only 5 objects. Encourage the children to use only the top cells in the 10s frame. Have children use less than 5 objects and ask how many more they will need to fill each of the cells in the top row. As children respond, write the progression from concrete to symbolic.

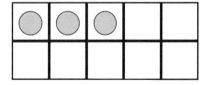

verbal: three counters and two make/is five counters
verbal/symbolic: 3 and 2 make 5
symbolic: 3 + 2 = 5

Have children play with the 10s frame and counters until they have constructed a variety of combinations to five.

Couple this exploration with subtraction number sentences. Ask children how many counters they would have if they had 5 and you asked them to give you 2. Model different ways to express this transaction. Talk with the children about how the equal sign can mean "make," "is," "left," "more," and so forth.

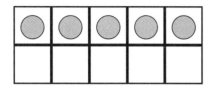

verbal: five counters, give away 2, leaves 3
verbal/symbolic: 5 give away 2 = 3
symbolic: 5 - 2 = 3

Once the children have reached their comfort level with 5, encourage them to show combinations, and then partitionings, for 10.

Sharing and Writing

Every time children show a different addition or subtraction activity, have them record the mathematics pictorially and then symbolically.

Encourage them to write a sentence or so about how they figured out the result. In some cases it might be as simple as, "I counted the empty squares."

Have children share examples with the class. The number sentences might be the same, but the solution processes will show many different strategies.

Activities with Tens Frames

How Many More, How Many Less?

Purpose: Visualize quantities to 10; basic facts to 10
Grouping of Students: Individual or pairs
Materials: 10 two-colored counters, 10s frames
NCTM Standards: Mathematics as Communication, Number Sense and Numeration, Whole Number Computation, Concepts of Whole Number Operations
Directions:
1. Have the children place from 1 to 5 counters on the frame and tell how many there are. Encourage the children to use one row at a time. As children become more accustomed to this activity, encourage them to use numerals.
2. After awhile, have children tell how many counters there are and then tell how many more they will need to have 5 in all. Have the children record how many they have and how many more are needed. You might want to model an addition or a subtraction sentence. For instance, 3 + *2* = 5, in which 2 is a missing addend, or

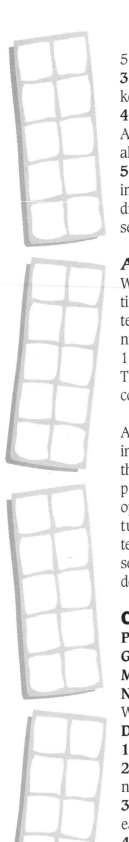

5 - 3 = *2*, in which the difference shows how many more are needed.

3. At a later time, have children work with 6 to 10 counters. Encourage children to keep a record of how they counted and how many they had each time.

4. After awhile, ask children how many more they would need to have 10 in all. Again, model for the children different ways they can show the counters using numerals and number sentences. For instance, 6 + *4* = 10 or 10 - 6 = *4*.

5. Increase the number of counters and 10s frames to include basic facts to 20. It is important to allow children sufficient time to internalize the different facts. The children also need to record the different facts pictorially, with accompanying number sentences.

Assessment

When children use the 10s frame with 5 or 10 counters, some will count from 1 every time. Others will visualize 5 counters and count on to get the total number. Still others will use 5 and 10 on the frames as benchmarks. They will either count on from 5 or count back from 10.

As you observe the children recording their investigations, you'll notice that some children will record using pictures and numbers but avoid operation signs. Others will use pictures and addition number sentences. Still others will use addition sentences and subtraction sentences, depending on questions asked.

Counting with Tens Frames

Purpose: Organize large quantities of counters
Grouping of Students: Individual or pairs
Materials: Bags with two-colored counters, 10s frames
NCTM Standards: Mathematics as Communication, Number Sense and Numeration, Whole Number Computation, Concepts of Whole Number Operations
Directions:
1. To each pair, give 1 bag and several 10s frames.
2. Have the children discuss how they might use the 10s frames to easily count the number of counters in the bag.
3. Have children use the counters and 10s frames to count the number of counters in each bag.
4. Ask children to record the number of counters and how they counted them.
5. Have them share their findings with the class. Does this way of organizing counting makes it easier to count a large number of counters?

Assessment

Some children will still count the total number of counters by 1. Others will count all the frames as if they were completely filled. For instance, instead of counting all the filled frames by 10 and then counting the last partially filled frame by 1, they will count that frame as 10. Still others will count the filled frames by 10 and the partially filled frame by 1.

Using Tens Frames for Recording Probability Experiments

Purpose: Explore probability and use 10s frames for recording

Grouping of Students: Pairs

Materials per pair: Shoe box with one corner cut off (Make the hole large enough for a snap cube to be partially seen, but not so big that the snap cube falls out. This enables the children to see the color of the snap cube.); tape; 1 red and 3 blue snap cubes; 10s frames, pencil and paper for recording

NCTM Standards: Mathematics as Problem Solving, Mathematics as Communication, Number Sense and Numeration, Probability and Statistics

Directions:

1. Place 1 red and 3 blue snap cubes in the shoe box.

2. Tape the lid to the box.

3. Give the pair a handful of blue and red snap cubes and two 10s frames.

4. Model the activity. Shake the box, then tilt it so that the color of one snap cube can be seen.

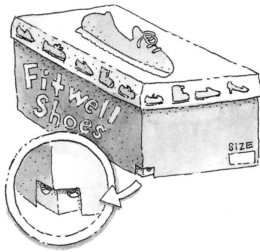

5. Have the children place that color snap cube on one of the 10s frames.

6. Repeat the activity.

7. Have the children do the activity with partners.

8. Have the children stop when one 10s frame is filled.

9. Record and share results.

10. How many red cubes and how many blue cubes do children think are in the box?

Assessment

As you observe the children doing the probability experiment, some will assume that there are the same number of blue and red cubes. Other children will assume that there are more blue cubes than red cubes. Still others will assume that the number of occurrences has something to do with the results but are not really clear on what the relationship is.

Clocks

Telling time on analog clocks is part of most mathematics curriculums in the primary grades. Young children can tell time to the hour and approximate time around the hour. Telling time, including minutes before and after the hour, is often confusing to children. They need much practice, and both teacher and child need patience.

Clocks as Manipulatives

The best manipulatives to use are the classroom clock and a set of stamps. The stamps should show the clock face of an analog clock and that of a digital clock.

There are also many different clocks available commercially on which children can manipulate the hands. These clocks should be used after children know how to tell time.

Telling Time to the Hour

When beginning instruction, focus on time to the hour and approximate time around the hour. Spending time on length of hands will help some children. But many youngsters visualize the placement of the hands, rather than length of the hands.

Start by asking the children to look at the classroom clock. What time do they think it is? (Begin this at the very beginning of the school day, then continue asking the same question every hour on the hour. Continue this pattern for several days and try to do it every time the clock shows exact time.)

As children describe the placement of the hands, they will begin to pay attention to the length of the clock hands. They will also see that the hour hand tells the time to the hour, while the minute hand is on 12.

Telling Approximate Time
As children become comfortable with telling time to the hour, introduce approximate time. When the classroom clock is 5 minutes to, or 5 minutes after the hour, ask what time it is.

Telling Time to the Half Hour
Telling time to the half hour is difficult for most children, since the hour hand is in-between hours. Often, telling quarter hours is easier, since the hour hand is closer to the hour.

Telling Time to the Quarter Hour
When the time is 15 minutes to the hour, tell children that it is 15 minutes to 10, for instance. An hour later, ask the children what time they think it is now. (Sometimes you might have to tell the time yourself, but frequently it does not take the children too much time to pick up on the pattern.)

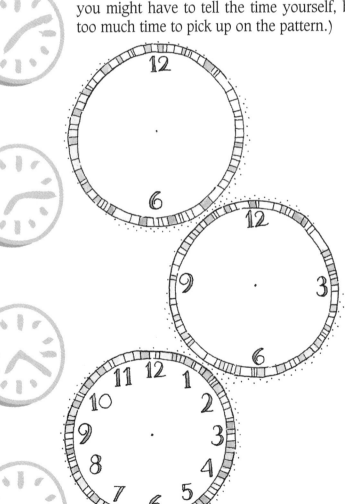

After introducing telling time to 15 minutes before the hour, ask questions related to time to the hour. Continue instruction with approximate time; that is, ask *about* what time it is. Follow the same steps with 15 minutes after the hour.

Each unit should include a cumulative lesson. That is, the children should have an opportunity to practice what they learned before the next concept is introduced.

MANAGEMENT TIP
To draw a clock, have the children trace a small circular object. Show them how they can place a tick mark for 12 at the top. Put the tick mark for 6 at the bottom. Do the same with 3 and 9. Children can place the other numerals approximately where they will fall on the clock face.

Writing and Sharing

Depending on the children's developmental level, instruction can proceed from telling time to the hour to telling time to the minute. In most cases, telling time to 5 minutes is all children in primary grades need. Encourage the children to write about what they have learned.

Digital Clocks

Since digital clocks show the time as it is recorded, they can be shown alongside analog clocks. Usually, young children's watches show time digitally.

If possible, invest in an inexpensive digital clock. These can often be purchased in discount drug stores for less than $2.00. Whenever children learn the concepts of telling time, ask a volunteer to record the way the time is recorded on the digital clock. Spend time on the clock notation, such as, "What does the colon mean? What does the first numeral tell? What do the two numerals after the colon tell? Why are some numerals preceded by zero?"

Maintaining Telling Time

Initial instruction on telling time will last for several months, although it will take only a few minutes each day. To maintain the children's knowledge, ask a few times a day what time it is.

Begin by asking the children *about* what time it is. This question will allow the participation of almost every child in the class. Then ask the children what the exact time is. Allow all the students an opportunity to agree or disagree.

The above activity lasts for as little as one minute. Tell the children that they have now spent *about one minute* on telling time. This gives the children an opportunity to pay attention to elapsed time.

Storing the Clocks

House small clocks in the package in which they were purchased. The colorful box will add a distinct color to the storage shelves. The name of the manipulative is already printed on the box.

If you have a set of clock stamps, keep them in a plastic container along with the stamp pad.

Activities with Clocks

Constructing Clocks

Purpose: Make telling time important by having each child construct his or her own clock faces

Grouping of Students: Individual

69

Materials: Thin, inexpensive paper plates; index cards, paper fasteners, crayons
NCTM Standards: Mathematics as Problem Solving, Mathematics as Communication, Whole Number Computation, Geometry and Spatial Sense
Directions:
1. Give each child a paper plate. Ask youngsters to fold the paper plate in half.
2. Ask children to open up the folded plate and place a tick mark at each edge of the fold.
3. Have the children fold the paper plate in half again, but match the previous folds before folding again.
4. Ask the children to open up the plate and place tick marks at the edge of the new fold. Then have them mark the center of the plate (the point where all the folds meet).
5. Have the children pick one of the tick marks and write 12 underneath it.
6. Have the children write a 6 opposite the 12.
7. Have the children place the plate in front of them, so that the 12 is on the top and the 6 on the bottom.
8. Ask youngsters to hold up their right hand and place a 3 on the right hand-side of the plate.
9. Have children place a 9 straight opposite the 3.
10. Ask children to fill in the remaining 8 numerals in the appropriate places.
11. Have the children decorate their clock faces.
12. Ask children to draw 2 clock hands on the index cards.
13. Help children punch holes in their clock hands and make a small hole in the center of the clock face.
14. Show the children how to assemble their clocks.
15. Encourage children to copy onto their clocks the placement of hands in the demonstration clock.

Assessment

Some children will find folding the paper plates in half difficult because they do not relate 1/2 to 2 parts. Other children have the general idea that 2 parts are needed to create halves, but they do not realize that they need 2 equal parts to make halves. Still other children match the edges to create halves.

When placing the remaining 8 numerals on the clock faces, some children do so without consideration to equal spacing. Others find placing the one-digit numerals less complicated than placing the 10 and the 11 on the clock face. Still others place tick marks for the missing numerals before writing the numerals themselves. Encourage the children to explain their plans before completing each task.

Using And Making Schedules

Purpose: Using their knowledge of time, children make daily schedules
Grouping of Students: Individual
Materials: Lined paper
NCTM Standards: Mathematics as Problem Solving, Mathematics as Communication, Whole Number Computation

Directions:

1. Give each child a piece of paper. Have the child fold it in half length-wise. Ask children to write TIME on the left-hand side and WHAT I DO on the right-hand side.

2. Have children write when they get up in the morning and what they do. Discuss with the children how long this activity lasts and show them how to write the time, for example 7-7:30 Breakfast.

3. Show children what their school schedule will look like. Have the children copy it from the board.

4. Have children continue working on their schedule at home. Their last entry for the day should read "Go to Bed."

5. Ask the children to write 3 problems concerning their schedule. After they have solved their problems on a separate piece of paper, have the children exchange their problems and solve their partner's problems. (For example, "I get up at 7 o'clock. I go to school at 8:30. How long am I awake before I go to school?")

6. Have the children talk about their solutions and the solution processes. How are they the same or different?

7. Create a class math book and include the problems in the math book. Divide the book into 2 parts: the first presents the math problems, the second includes the different solutions.

Assessment

Some children will stay entirely with time to the hour and will show only the time an activity begins. They will not note elapsed time. Other children will show time intervals, as well as time to the hour and half hour. Still other children will include times to the quarter hour and, sometimes, time to 5-minute intervals.

Sixty Minutes as a Number Line

Purpose: Show how minutes are related to the hours on an analog clock
Grouping of Students: Whole group
Materials: Thick yarn or heavy string, about 80-72 inches for the clock and 8 additional inches to tie the string into a circle; index cards; permanent markers; masking tape
NCTM Standards: Mathematics as Problem Solving, Mathematics as Communication, Whole Number

71

Computation, Number Sense and Numeration, Measurement

Directions:

1. Have groups of children write the numerals 5 through 60 (minutes), in increments of 5. That is, 5, 10, 15, 20, 25, etc. Ask the children to place the cards vertically before writing the numerals.

2. With the children's help, place masking tape markers every 6 inches. (Put the first marker four inches from the beginning.)

3. Have children tape the index cards to the string, starting with 5. Line up the card with one edge touching a masking tape marker. Tape the string so that the bottoms of the cards touch the string.

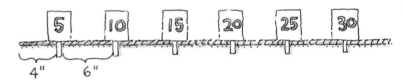

4. Have the children look at the number line they have created. Have children walk the number line, counting as they walk.

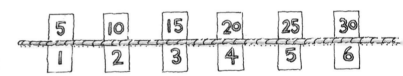

5. Then have groups of children write the numerals 1 through 12 (hours).

6. Place the number line on the floor. Tape the second set of numerals underneath the numerals representing minutes.

7. Tie the ends of the strings together to form a circle.

8. Place the circle on the floor so that the cards representing minutes are protruding outside the yarn circle and the cards showing hours are on the inside of the yarn circle. Have children talk about how this circle reminds them of a clock.

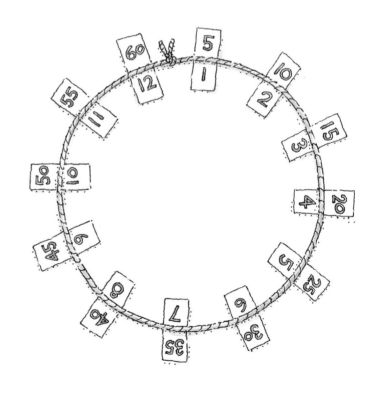

9. Concentrate on the minutes.

72

Talk with the children about where the clock hand would be placed if the time was, for instance, 20 minutes after an hour. Continue with this type of questioning before involving the hour.

10. Once the children are comfortable with minutes, concentrate on the placement of the hour hand.

11. Have children note how the hour hand changes its position during the progression from one hour to the next.

12. Use only one specific hour during the initial explorations of time-telling to 5-minute intervals. For instance, if math time is between 10 and 11, use these two times to tell time to 5-minute accuracy.

13. Have boys and girls practice their knowledge throughout the day and for days to come.

Assessment

Some children can place the minute hand correctly, but will always place the hour hand on the hour called for, regardless of the minutes that are involved. For instance, they will show 10:45 with the minute hand on 45 but the hour hand on 10. Others will place the hour hand correctly when showing time on the hour as well as half past, but will be less clear when showing times that exceed 30 minutes. Still others will show the hour hand on the hour for 5 to 25 minutes after the hour; in between the 2 hours involved when showing 30 to 40 minutes; and on the following hour when showing 45 minutes to the hour.

Money

Most commercially available plastic coins are more expensive than real money and, in most cases, do not have the detail that real money has. The collections that can be bought include one or two coins that children seldom see or use on a daily basis. Therefore, whenever possible, use real coins. Have on hand a collection of change that children can use for lessons on an ongoing basis.

For dollar bills, though, it makes sense to use play money. They are inexpensive and their monetary values are printed on the bills. Ask volunteers or the PTA to contribute a variety of change for lessons.

Different Denominations

Using money is fascinating to most children. The mathematics inherent in these lessons makes these activities valuable developmentally to the children. Because of the abstract nature of money, using coins and bills in the classroom helps children make connections between the concrete and the symbolic.

Convention dictates why a nickel is worth 5¢, a dime 10¢. Children should become familiar with the look and feel of different coins.

Young children enjoy making books of different coins, in which they record physical attributes of the coins. (For example, the penny has a different color than the rest of the coins. Its edge has no ridges. It is the second smallest coin. It is called one cent.

One cent can be written 1¢. Some children will also include descriptions of the illustrations on the coins.) Older children might get involved in doing rubbings of the coins.

Combinations

After the children have spent time on the physical attributes and value of the different coins, have them use coins to show various combinations that equal the value of a quarter.

Writing and Sharing

Have children record their combinations. They can start out with sheets of paper and staple them together along the side to form a booklet. They can also make a booklet at the beginning of the unit and use a page for each combination. Have the children talk about how many pages they think they will need or how many different combinations show the value of a quarter.

Adding and Subtracting

Activities with money lend themselves to adding and subtracting with a purpose. When it comes to money, children have few problems with multi-digit addition and subtraction.

MANAGEMENT TIP

If some of the children feel frustrated because they have only the obvious combinations, such as 25 pennies, 5 nickels, 2 dimes and 1 nickel, focus their attention on the last combination. Ask them to show another way to make 25¢. This time they need to use more nickels, but only one dime. Then ask them to show 25¢ by using some pennies, nickels, and dimes. Before the children proceed, talk with them about how they can use this way of organizing the information to keep track of what they have done and what else they can do.

Keep the coins and bills available for use throughout different activities. They help children count and organize their solution processes, even though money, in itself, is abstract.

If lunch money is collected weekly or each morning, make this activity the responsibility of the students.

In the beginning of the school year, have partners figure out the total when they add their amounts. Then combine groups of four. Have them figure out how much money they have altogether and tell what strategy they used to count it. Continue combining groups, but keep the basic group of four to get manageable subtotals. Assign different students the responsibility of reporting the group's total. During early lessons, use the whole class to record and add the class total. Eventually, assign pairs the responsibility of adding the group's subtotals.

Other Activities

Make up story problems that include the whole class or individual students. Take the whole class or individuals on an imaginary shopping trip to the supermarket or toy store. Tell about a purchase and how it is paid for. Ask the children if there is any change. How much? How did they figure it out?

Storing Coins and Bills

Store the materials in individual plastic lunch bags that can be zipped closed. Share the available coins in such a way that there is a bag of coins for each pair of children. If possible, each bag should contain 2 quarters, 2 dimes, 5 nickels, 5 pennies, and a fake dollar bill. Write the content on the bags. Store all the bags in a box.

MANAGEMENT TIP
Since coins can roll off desks or become misplaced, assign each pair of students one bag that they will use throughout the school year. Have the children count the contents when they first receive the bag and check it against the listed contents. Have them repeat this activity before and after each lesson. Have them record the date at the end of each lesson. This gives them a reason to record the date.

Activities with Money

Money Puzzles

Purpose: Recognize money through verbal descriptions
Grouping of Students: Whole group
Materials: Various coins
NCTM Standards: Mathematics as Problem Solving, Mathematics as Communication, Mathematics as Reasoning, Number Sense and Numeration, Whole Number Computation
Directions:
1. Model the game for the children.
2. Take two or three coins, count the total value of the coins, and hide your hand behind your back or place your hand in a pocket.
3. Tell the number of coins you have in your hand.
4. Ask the children to identify the coins after asking "yes" and "no" questions. They are allowed 10 questions in all.
5. The child with the correct answer leads the next activity.

Assessment

Some children will ask specific questions such as, "Do you have any pennies?" Other children will ask broader questions such as, "Do the coins have edges with ridges?" Still others will ask questions that are broad, but that also add information from which they can narrow down to a specific answer: "Do you have more than 50¢?"

Shopping Spree

Purpose: Compare and assign prices to different objects represented in catalogs

Grouping of Students: Individual or pairs

Materials: Catalogs, magazines, and store flyers, glue sticks, large sheets of construction paper

NCTM Standards: Mathematics as Problem Solving, Mathematics as Communication, Mathematics as Reasoning, Number Sense and Numeration, Whole Number Computation

Directions:

1. Tell the children that they are going to create their own catalog business and their own catalogs.

2. Have children cut out pictures from catalogs and glue them onto construction paper. Have the children name their catalog business.

3. Tell the children to assign a price for each item. The prices can range from 10¢ to $1.

4. Display the children's catalogs around the room.

5. Then have the children create a purchase list for themselves. They will have $1 to spend and will decide how to spend their money.

6. Give the children an opportunity to go shopping. Remind them to look at the different catalog sheets before deciding on their purchases. Have the children list their purchases and the costs.

7. Invite children to tell what they bought, how much money they spent, and how much money they have left.

8. Have the children write about their purchases, telling how and why they made their decisions.

Assessment

Observe how children assign prices to the products they "sell." Some children will assign a value of $1 to all their products, because that way they will "get the most money." Others will assign values of 50¢ to $1 for their products. They will not consider the real objects, but the size of the picture. Still others will vary their prices, taking into consideration the real object the picture represents. (A car is more expensive than a bicycle.)

Fractions, Decimals, And Language

Purpose: Connect children's everyday language to fractions and decimals
Grouping of Students: Pairs
Materials: 4 quarters and dollar bills
NCTM Standards: Mathematics as Problem Solving, Mathematics as Communication, Mathematics as Reasoning, Number Sense and Numeration, Whole Number Computation, Fractions and Decimals, Patterns and Relationships
Directions:

1. Have children use 1 quarter, draw a picture of it, and write 25¢ underneath.

2. Have children brainstorm what a quarter means (beside 25¢), such as 1/4.

3. Have the children tell how many quarters make $1.

4. Connect that a quarter is 1 out of 4 with the symbolic notation 1/4. Tell the children that one quarter is another name for 1/4.

5. Have the children show the fraction notation underneath the picture drawn earlier.

6. Show the children that 25¢ can also be written $0.25.

7. Have the children use 2 quarters, draw a picture of the coins, and write 50¢ underneath.

8. Ask the children if they know another name for 50¢.

9. Connect the words "Half a dollar" to the symbolic notation 1/2. Have the children write 1/2 underneath the picture. How many half dollars make up 1 dollar?

10. Show that 50¢ can be written $0.50.

11. Repeat the activity with three quarters.

Assessment

Some children will avoid the fraction and decimal symbols. They will use the cent-notation. Others will use without difficulty the word names for the fractions and the decimal notation. Still others will use the fraction, the decimal notation, and the whole number notation with cents.

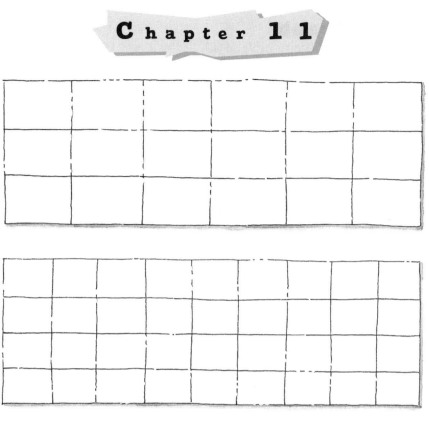

Floor Mats

Floor mats are made of heavy plastic. They have printed grids on both sides. They are great to use when creating physical graphs. The mats provide an opportunity for young children to move from the physical graphs to representational picture graphs. Thus, children can graph objects such as shoes, fruit, toys, and pictures they have drawn of objects that they cannot bring to school.

Labeling The Graph

There is little reason to number the axes of the graph because the size of each cell makes counting an easy task. Young children tend to rely on counting rather than the more difficult task of looking for the intersection of the horizontal and vertical lines. The size of the mats, as well as the cell size, allows children to use visual comparison as they interpret the information on the graph. The axis that uses groups of some kind, such as fruit, footwear, patterns, etc., needs to be labeled.

In the beginning, you might want each child to decide where to put the object or the pictorial representation. But before interpreting the graph the bars should be labeled, especially if they have chosen a color to represent an object or an idea. For example, look at the activity on page 85. It deals with the patterns on the soles of children's shoes. Without a label for each bar, it would be impossible to determine what the bar stands for.

Naming the Graph

Encourage children to give their graphs a title. (This helps youngsters in the future, as graph titles become important when deciding what information they want to show.) Since most graphing activities in primary grades are teacher-initiated, the titles of the graphs help children take ownership of the information. The title then becomes a part of the general discussion on how and why to graph.

Counting and Comparing

Once the children have created a visual display, it is important that they look at the information they have compiled. What does the graph tell them? Usually there is a preference shown. Here children have an opportunity to talk informally about the *mode* of their graph; that is, the most frequently occurring event.

Children can also look at the number relationships involved. If there are 30 students and 17 prefer oranges and grapefruit, then about half of the class prefer citrus fruit. If 19 out of 30 students like pizza, then more than half, or almost 2/3, of the children like pizza. Obviously, the sophistication of the fractions will depend on the age of the children and their background with fractional relationships.

Writing and Sharing

After the children have discussed the graph in a whole group, ask them to tell what information they find most interesting and why. Have the children copy the graph. Encourage them to write a few summarizing sentences. In their writing, have children mention what they liked about the graph.

Storing the Floor Mats

The floor mats should be stored in some kind of storage bag because plastic has a tendency to attract dust and they will seem dirty.

They can be cleaned with any glass cleaner, but this, at times, becomes burdensome. The mats can be stored folded or rolled, depending on storage space. Do not use any kind of markers on the plastic, whether water-based or dry-erase. The markers will not wipe off.

Activities with Floor Mats

Shoes, Sneakers, and Boots

Purpose: Display information

Grouping of Students: Whole class

Materials: Floor mats, children's footwear, index cards

NCTM Standards: Mathematics as Problem Solving, Mathematics as Communication, Mathematics as Reasoning, Number Sense and Numeration, Whole Number Computation, Patterns and Relationships, Statistics and Probability

Directions:

1. Ask the children, one at a time, to place their footwear on the grid.

2. Ask the children why they placed their shoes in a particular bar.

3. If the class is so large that the floor mat is not long enough, use masking tape on the floor to add cells.

4. Have the children label the bars using index cards.

5. Have children decide how many students there are in school that particular day.

6. Ask the children what is the most common footwear. How do they know? How many are wearing this type of footwear? About what fraction of the entire class is that? More than half? Less than half?

7. Have the children decide on a title for the graph.

8. Have children summarize their findings and record them.

Assessment

As children are interpreting the graph, some children will acknowledge the most common footwear, if they are also

> **MANAGEMENT TIP**
>
> Do this activity when children do not have gym, a special assembly, or an event scheduled that would call for specific footwear.

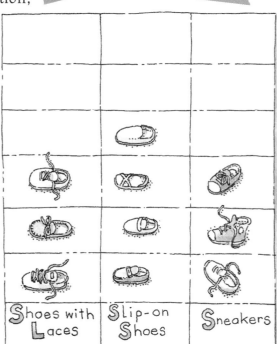

> **MANAGEMENT TIP**
>
> Have children remove only one of their shoes or sneakers. This will help them identify the mate at the end of the activity. If many children seem to have the same type of footwear, write each child's name on a piece of masking tape and have them attach their name to the shoe before beginning the activity.

wearing that particular footwear. Others will report the numbers of the different bars. Still others will talk about the most commonly worn footwear, tell how many more than the next common item, and include the least common item.

Favorite Fruits

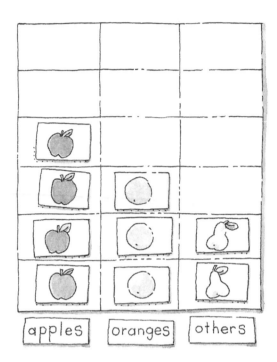

Purpose: Make a graph, using pictures to represent the objects, and label the horizontal axis; include a general group labeled "Other"

Grouping of Students: Whole group

Materials: Index cards for labels and the title of the bar graph; construction paper for drawing; crayons or markers

NCTM Standards: Mathematics as Problem Solving, Mathematics as Communication, Mathematics as Reasoning, Number Sense and Numeration, Whole Number Computation, Patterns and Relationships, Statistics and Probability

Directions:

1. Begin a discussion about the fruit children most like to eat.

2. Ask each child to draw a picture of his or her favorite fruit.

3. Have children place their picture where they think it belongs.

4. Have the children place outside the floor mat the fruit that does not belong in any bar.

5. After all the pictures have been placed, have the children decide on labels for each bar. For example, Citrus fruit, Apples, Green fruit, Yellow fruit, Fruit with sections, etc.

6. Have the children check to see if any of the fruits outside the floor mat could be placed in any of the labeled bars.

7. If there are still pictures that do not belong to any bar, have the children grapple with what to call that bar.

8. After children have named the last category, have them interpret the data.

9. Ask the children which fruit is the favorite fruit. The children will determine that by the length of the bar. Have the children count how many children like that particular fruit, for example, 15 children. Then have them figure out how many children are in the class, for example, 32. Have them name the fraction 15/32, which is approximately 1/2.

Assessment

Some children will copy the number of pictures in each bar. The pictures will not necessarily be aligned with other bars, but each bar will have the correct number in it. They summarize the information by giving the number of children who like the different fruits.

Other children will align the pictures in each bar and illustrate each cell, even though the illustrations cannot be seen because of their size. The children will report on the favorite and least favorite fruit of the class, if the data is available. Still other children will create a bar graph using the picture graph as its reference. They will label each bar and use squares for each vote. They will align the bars. They will report on the number of people who like the different fruits but also give the corresponding fractions of the class's favorite fruit.

Keeping Track of Patterns on Soles

Purpose: Use color to distinguish categories
Grouping of Students: Whole class
Materials: Floor mat, shoes/sneakers, colored construction-paper squares, index cards

NCTM Standards: Mathematics as Problem Solving, Mathematics as Communication, Mathematics as Reasoning, Number Sense and Numeration, Whole Number Computation, Patterns and Relationships, Statistics and Probability
Directions:
1. Have the children look at the different patterns on the soles of their shoes and sneakers and decide on categories of these patterns.
2. Ask the children to narrow the categories to three or four patterns, such as straight or wavy lines, swirls or circles, combinations of straight lines and swirls, and smooth (no lines).
3. Invite children to write the categories on index cards and place the labels underneath the columns of the floor mat graph.

4. Ask them to assign a color to represent each pattern and decide what pattern they have on the soles of their footwear.
5. Ask them to place their colored squares in the appropriate columns.
6. Have the children interpret the data on the graphs. How is this information displayed differently from the physical and picture graphs created earlier?
7. Give children sheets of squared or graph paper to copy the graphs. Encourage them to write a report on the data.

Assessment

As children talk about the difference between the physical, pictorial, and representational bar graphs, some children will find the color representation of a pattern confusing. They will refer to the color, rather than the pattern on the soles of the shoes.

Other children will talk about their own patterns, referring to the colors they used.

Still other children will use the patterns in their descriptions, rather than the color of the bars.

Chapter 12

Summing-Up

Young children need to experience most subjects physically, at least to some degree. Therefore, it is important that children have an opportunity to explore mathematics using manipulatives. It is also important that they are given ample time for their explorations. This will allow them to do the activity in depth and make the necessary connections to mathematical expressions and symbolic notations.

Mathematics All Around

Whenever you have an opportunity to connect mathematics to children's everyday lives, you will find that many more of the children participate in the activity. For example, counting is one of the most important activities in primary grade mathematics. Counting helps children develop a one-to-one correspondence, recognize cardinality, and begin to comprehend quantity.

If anything needs to be counted in the classroom, have the children do so. Let the children count
- the light bulbs in the room
- shoes and shoelaces
- hands
- fingers
- number of steps from children's desks to where they line up in class
- number of steps they take when they go to lunch
- different manipulatives in the classroom

These counting activities allow *all* children in the class to participate. It does not matter whether they speak English, as long as they know the numbers and understand the concept of counting.

Shopping is another activity children like to do. Most children can perform sophisticated mental computing with money, which they might not be able to do with paper and pencil. Youngsters know that 2 quarters make 50¢ and 2 dimes and a nickel make a quarter, but find it difficult to do $25 + 25$ and $10 + 10 + 5$.

When starting the children on different shopping sprees, make up a few problems using some of the children's names. Then give them a few pages from a store flyer or catalog. Ask them to make up their own problems. Have the children solve their problems on separate pieces of paper. That way they can share the problems with the class or a partner. When classmates have solved their problems, they can share their solutions and solution processes.

The pages can be assembled into classroom mathematics books to be kept on the class library shelf. At the end of the school year, have your class write some mathematics books for the next school year's incoming class. The children can include for the new students some personal messages and feelings about math.

When there are some free moments in the daily routine, use the time to give the children math problems. For instance, if the class is waiting for the special-subject teacher to pick them up, have the children estimate how many pages there are in a book, how many crayons in a can, how many counters in a container, or how many snap cubes in a rod. Count the objects aloud with the class. This will give them an idea of the correctness of their estimates, as well as practice using the number words.

Always encourage the children to agree or disagree with the different responses. Have them explain why they agree or disagree. These types of activities give the children immediate feedback, and an opportunity to self-correct their responses.

Mathematics needs to be an ongoing activity in the classroom. Sometimes you might give children information that they did not have previously. This information can give rise to research by the children. For instance, when you open a package of construction paper, tell them that this is a ream of paper and that a ream contains 500 pieces of paper. Ask them if they know words that refer to specific or approximate numbers. Most of the children know that a dozen stands for 12. Do they know how many wolves are in a pack of wolves or how many lions are in a pride of lions?

Mathematics Throughout the Curriculum

A typical school day contains many opportunities for using mathematics informally. In reading, the children encounter many pieces of literature and stories that can expand their understanding of mathematics. Some books have clear-cut references to numbers and operations, while others do not.

In Pat Hutchin's *Rosie's Walk,* children can move into Discrete Mathematics by talking about different combinations of Rosie's path. How many ways can she begin and end up in the same place? Are any of the paths they come up with duplications? Does the path remain the same length, or does the distance change?

Children can also talk about the patterns of page numbers. Is the left-hand page always an even number? Can they predict if page 45 is going to be on the left-hand side or the right-hand side? What about the illustrations? How many windows might the illustrated building have in all? How did they figure it out? Did they only consider the face of the building that is illustrated, or did they also consider the sides and the back of the building? In this instance, children use their previous or everyday knowledge.

Science is another subject that provides many opportunities for mathematics. In most schools, primary school children will grow plants from seeds. Measuring the plants gives rise to wonderful opportunities for keeping track of the plants' growth. Youngsters can then display the growth using a graph.

Whatever the subject, mathematics can and should be integrated into other subjects in the same way as reading and writing is integrated into mathematics. Some activities,

such as telling time, will be more successful if done throughout the school day.

Asking Questions

Always encourage children to talk about their experiences with manipulatives. At times, asking questions might seem difficult. To get started in the questioning routine, you need to remember only two questions. These are: "Can you tell me about what you have done?" and "What other ways could you solve the problem?"

The first question will help you find out where the child is in his or her understanding of the problem. As the child explains, you might find out about strategies you want shared with the rest of the class. If there are any misunderstandings in the child's perception, they will also become apparent at this time.

The second question will show the child's conceptual understanding of the problem. In some cases, the children might choose to use a calculator to show the solution another way. This clearly shows that the children are comfortable with the symbolic notations because they must use the correct symbolism on the calculator.

Sometimes, writing on a large piece of paper "good" questions that children ask each other can be helpful. Post it prominently in the classroom. A "question" poster might also come in handy if *you* cannot think of a good question to ask.

Finding Opportunities to Modify, Challenge, and Extend Mathematics

All of the activities listed in this book can be modified or extended by changing the quantities. Make the quantity smaller if the children find the suggested quantities frustrating. Make it larger if the children need more of a challenge.

Once the children have reached a comfort level with symbolic notation, you can help them see the inverse relationship between addition and subtraction. This can be done most effectively by having children see patterns between addition and subtraction number sentences. You might want to show a complete example of related number sentences, such as the following:

$$4 + 5 = 9 \qquad 5 + 4 = 9$$
$$9 - 5 = 4 \qquad 9 - 4 = 5$$

Ask the children what they can say about the four sentences. How are they "related?" If they know that $4 + 5 = 9$, how could they solve $9 - 5 = ?$

Although these relationships are obvious to adults, they are not self-evident to children. Spend ample time talking about the example before adding other number sentences. You might also want to return to simpler activities or smaller quantities to help children visualize this relationship. The activity STAIRCASE PATTERNS FOR ADDITION AND SUBTRACTION (pp. 18–19) can also be used at this time.

All the different properties of addition and subtraction can be explored using manipulatives. For instance, addition is commutative, but subtraction is not. Children can add quantities in any order and it will not change the total. They cannot subtract quantities in any order and still get the same difference. Encourage children to talk about the identity property quite early; that is, adding and subtracting zero will leave the original quantity unchanged.

Whenever the children are involved in any mathematical activities, ask them to generalize about their findings. For instance, when dealing with the area of a surface, encourage them to explore different-sized units. Then encourage them to generalize about the relationship between the number of units needed depending on the size of the unit.

Easy, Inexpensive Ways to Make or Obtain Manipulatives

Sometimes school resources are limited and you must choose which school supplies to purchase. Some manipulatives, such as snap cubes or links, cannot be made using household items. You might want to order these from commercial sources. Other items, such as two-colored counters or floor mats, can be made inexpensively from household items.

Two-Colored Counters

Use one or two bags of large lima beans and a can of spray paint in any color you desire. In a well-ventilated area, put down some old newspapers or other type of disposable material. Cover the newspaper with a single layer of lima beans. Place the beans slightly apart. Spray paint the beans on one side with the color you have chosen. Let them dry overnight. These can now be used in the same way as two-colored counters.

Geometric Solids

Save a variety of packaging materials. Cover the containers with construction paper in different colors or spray paint. Since the most commonly used packaging shapes are

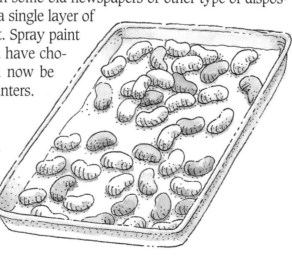

boxes and a cans, you will have plenty of rectangular prisms and cylinders. Balls make wonderful spheres, which cannot be effectively constructed out of paper. Cones and pyramids are not that common and you might need to construct these.

Party hats make wonderful cones, but be sure to add a base to the hat in order to make it a geometric solid or a three-dimensional object. If party hats are unavailable, use inexpensive paper plates. The diameter of the plate is usually given on the package. Divide the diameter in half, measure and mark that distance on the plate, and draw a straight line from the edge to the center. Cut along the line. Overlap the cut edges until you get the size of cone you like. Staple the bottom edge along the overlap and tape the edges that the stapler does not reach. Use the cone as a stencil and make a base for the shape. Tape the base to the cone.

Pyramids can be constructed using poster board. Draw four identical triangles with a 4" base and tape the sides together. Then draw a 4" square. Cut out the square and tape it as a base to the triangles.

Geoboards

Use 6" x 6" cut wood boards. Most lumber yards will cut these free if you tell them that you are going to use them for the school children. Give the lumberyard ample time. They will usually cut these boards from scrap pieces during down-time, when they're not busy.

Use 1" squared paper. Cut a 6" square and place the paper on top of a piece of wood. Use 3/4" thin nails with rounded heads and hammer a nail at each intersection, starting 1" from each edge. Remove the paper. You will have five rows of five nails.

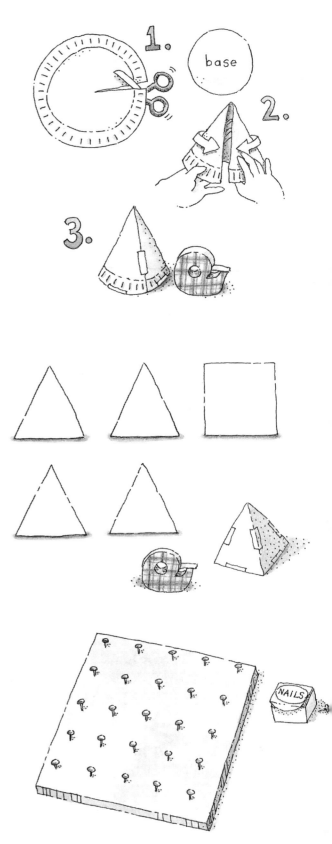

94

Buy a small bag of different-sized rubber bands. They usually cost less than one dollar. One bag is enough for four to five geoboards. You might want to keep these rubber bands in a small lunch bag that zips closed or in a small plastic container.

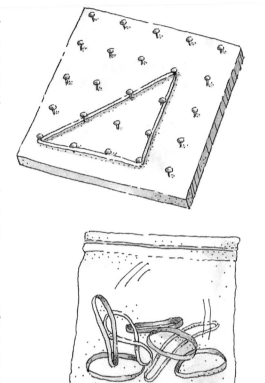

Floor Mats

Floor mats can be made from white shower curtain liners—the heavier the shower curtain liner, the longer the floor mat will last. Cut the shower curtain in half. You will have 2 pieces of plastic, each approximately 36" x 72".

You may also use a painters' drop cloth for the floor mat. Because this is made of cloth, you can paint the grid on it. The drop cloth will last much longer and folds easier than a plastic floor mat. Drop cloths come in different sizes, but you do not need the floor mat to be larger than approximately 3', or 36", wide. You can make it as long as the drop cloth, but it needs to be at least 72" long. You might want to cut the drop cloth to size and use the leftover cloth for other purposes. Both grids can be painted on one piece of cloth, one grid on one side and the other grid on the other side.

Use black electrical tape to make the grid. If you want a more colorful grid, use heavy plastic decorator tape. Tape all the edges by folding the tape over the edge, framing the mat on both sides. Divide the width of the mat into three sections. Then mark the length of the mat into 12" sections. Place the tape over each mark so that the mark falls in the middle of the tape. This mat will have a grid that is 3' x 6'.

Take the other plastic piece, and again, frame the piece with tape. Divide the width into 4 sections. Then mark the mat into 8" sections lengthwise. Again place the tape over each mark, so that the mark falls in the middle of the tape. This mat will have a 4' x 9' grid.

When you need to expand the classroom inventory of manipulatives, involve the children in making or collecting these materials. All children can contribute to the classroom collection. By involving children, they feel empowered. They also feel ownership of their classroom materials and will be more careful using and storing all the supplies.

BIBLIOGRAPHY

Burns, M. *About Teaching Mathematics.* Sausalito, CA: Math Solutions Publications, 1992.

Carey, D. A. "Number Sentences: Linking Addition And Subtraction Word Problems And Symbols." *Journal For Research in Mathematics Education*, Volume 22, pages 266-280.

Charles, R. I. and E. A. Silver (eds.). *The Teaching and Assessing of Mathematical Problem Solving.* Hillsdale, NJ: Lawrence Erlbaum Associates, 1989.

Cooney, T. J. and C. R. Hirsch (eds.). *Teaching and Learning Mathematics in the 1990s.* Reston, VA: National Council of Teachers of Mathematics, 1990.

Eves, Howard. *An Introduction to the History of Mathematics.* Philadelphia, PA: Saunders College Publishing, 1990.

Gelman, R. and C. S. Gallistel. *The Child's Understanding of Number.* Cambridge, MA: Harvard University Press, 1978.

Ginsburg, H. P. *Children's Arithmetic: How They Learn It and How You Teach It.* Austin, TX: Pro Ed, 1989.

Ginsburg, H. P. and Joyce Baron. "Cognition: Young Children's Construction of Mathematics." In Robert J. Jensen (ed.) *Research Ideas for the Classroom: Early Childhood Mathematics.* New York: Macmillan Publishing Co., 1993.

Greeno, J. G. "Number Sense As Situated Knowing in A Conceptual Domain." *Journal For Research in Mathematics Education.* 1991, Volume 22, pages 170-218.

Hiebert, J. and Diana Wearne. "Links Between Teaching and Learning Place Value with Understanding in First Grade." *Journal For Research In Mathematics Education.* Volume 21, 1992, pages 98-122.

Jensen, R. J. (ed.). *Early Childhood Mathematics; Research Ideas for the Classroom.* New York: Macmillan Publishing Co., 1993.

Johnson, D. W. and R. J. Johnson. *Circles of Learning, Cooperation in the Classroom.* Alexandria, VA: Association for Supervision and Curriculum Development, 1984.

—*Learning Together and Alone.* Englewood Cliffs, NJ: Prentice Hall, 1987.

Kamii, C. K. *Young Children Continue to Reinvent Arithmetic: Implications of Piaget's Theory.* New York: Teachers College Press, 1990.

Kamii, C. K. *Young Children Reinvent Arithmetic: Implications of Piaget's Theory.* New York: Teachers College Press, 1985.

Kaput, J. J. "Technology and Mathematics Education." In D. A. Grouws (ed) *Handbook of Research On Mathematics Teaching and Learning.* New York: Macmillan Publishing Co., 1992.

National Council of Teachers of Mathematics. *Curriculum and Evaluation Standards for School Mathematics.* Reston, VA: 1989.

National Council of Teachers of Mathematics. *Professional Standards for Teaching Mathematics,* Reston, VA: 1991.

Payne, J. N. (ed.) *Mathematics for The Young Child,* Reston, VA: NCTM, 1990.

Piaget, J. *The Child's Conception of Number.* London: Routledge and Kegan Paul, 1952.

Piaget, J. *To Understand Is to Invent: The Future of Education.* New York: Grossman, 1973.

Stenmark, J. K. *Assessment Alternatives in Mathematics.* Berkeley, CA: Lawrence Hall of Science, 1989.

Zaslavsky, Claudia. *Africa Counts.* Brooklyn, NY: Lawrence Hill Books, 1979.